YOU ARE THE

Mother
Your Children Need

Joy on the Journey!
~Christie Gardiner

YOU ARE THE

Mother

Your Children Need

BELIEVING IN YOUR GOD-GIVEN GIFTS, TALENTS, AND ABILITIES

CHRISTIE GARDINER

Covenant Communications, Inc.

For my best friend and dearest love,
Doug

For the children who made me a mother:
Hailey, Elisabeth, and Christian

And for the woman who always said, "Yes, you can!"
For you, Mom

Table of Contents

Prologue
I See You

Dear Friend,

I need you to know I see you. I see you because I *am* you. You may drive a different mommy-mobile than I do. Our kids may be different ages or genders. Your children might be grown, or you may be just beginning, whereas I am smack-dab in the middle. You might consider yourself to be struggling with money, or you might be financially set for life. Maybe you work outside the home; maybe you don't. But none of that matters. We are one. We sit together in the carpool lane of solidarity in our divine, awesome, and totally overwhelming mission of raising up daughters and sons of God!

I know this is a hard job. I know you haven't had a shower today—maybe not yesterday either. I know at times you wonder why you said good-bye to so many of your dreams and ambitions so you could change six thousand nine hundred thirty-two diapers per child (I did the math)! I know croup scares you. I know you are tired and your best day last week was the day you got six whole, uninterrupted hours of sleep. I know you used to be fearless, but now every story on the news feels as if it is happening to you because you are a mother. And I know thinking about your divine role of mother leaves you timid and vulnerable with everything inside you exposed.

But I also know . . .

That at night—no matter how exhausted you are—you look at your sleeping child and your heart physically hurts with love. So much so that as you look at a tiny toe poking out of a hole in your child's footie pajamas, you are reverentially aware that there is nothing closer to God than being the mom of the owner of that little toe.

I know you worry that you aren't enough. How could you possibly be? There are so many things to do right, and your list of ineptitudes seems overwhelming. But I have to tell you something, and I need you to listen: The woman you want to be . . . the one who has within her every talent, gift, and ability to be what her children need? She's already there.

She is you.

Our Father in Heaven prepared you specifically for this time, in this place, with these children. You *are* the mother your children need.

> The woman you want to be . . . the one who has within her every talent, gift, and ability to be what her children need? She's already there. She is you.

Chapter 1
Show Up As You with God

In the writing world, we have a literary tradition we call "the six-word story."[1] In a nutshell, it is a writer's entire story summed up in six words. And so I give you this entire book about being the mother your children need in six words.

Show up as *you* with God.

There. That's it. Now you can put the book down and hide in the tub while you pretend to be reading it. Feel free to hide your latest regency romance in the middle of these pages instead. Everyone will think you are reading a book to improve your mothering skills. They'll be so impressed.

If we could really get it from those six words, we'd be set. The problem is most of us believe there is more to it. We don't believe we are enough. We

1 https://en.wikipedia.org/wiki/Six-Word_Memoirs.

need help understanding that all our children really need from their mother is for her to show up in authenticity, hand in hand with God.

When I was a brand-new mother, I attended a weeknight Relief Society meeting on the topic of motherhood. It was called homemaking meeting back then. I felt like a little baby-bird mommy amongst all the wise-owl mothers. Young and eager to learn, I had my notebook on my lap, poised to take copious notes on how to be a mom. A woman I greatly admired was speaking. She was fourteen years further along in this business of mothering and was, in my mind, the epitome of motherhood. She gave a warm, encouraging talk, and at the end of her speech, she said, "You are the mother your children need."

I don't remember much of the talk before these words, nor do I remember much of what came after. The notes taken that night have long since disappeared into the black hole of a house with two adults, three children, and a dog, but the memory remains. Those seven spoken words seared themselves onto my soul and the imprint is still here. "You are the mother your children need."

I have used these words as an anthem cry in my various motherhood battles ever since. While facing off for twenty-plus minutes with a three-year-old over whether he actually has to eat his vegetables, I say to myself, "Sister, you are stronger than this child's attitude. I know you just want to give in so he can go to bed and you can binge-watch the latest PBS special while eating the cake you hid in a plastic container behind the health food in the pantry, but do not give in! This kid needs his veggies, and he needs you to help him realize this. You are the mother your children need!"

I have used these words when I've been afraid in the middle of the night, holding a bundled up, sick baby, going back and forth between a steamy bathroom and cold outside air, all the while watching this precious baby struggle to breathe and understanding the reality of mortality as I never have before. I silently cry, "You will get through this. You know she belongs to God and is in His care. You do your best, and the rest *has* to be His. You are the mother your children need."

I have used these words in joy as I've watched my little son play with his toys, knowing the fight it was to bear that child. His smile lights up as he bangs his Matchbox cars together in the warm sunlight coming through his window. "Look at that boy! You did it! You had him, and now look—here he is happy and healthy. You are the mother your children need."

I have used these words in total shock upon finding out my own fourth-grade daughter was one of the elementary school's highly-sought-after serial vandals. I have had to buoy myself up with the words, "Yes, your child has defaced the school by turning on all the faucets in all of the bathrooms, causing flooding and mass PTA hysteria, but you are still a good mother. You didn't teach her to do that, but now you get to teach her about agency, accountability, and consequences. You are the mother your children need!"

I have used these words as a victory cry as I've watched my daughter (the vandal, by the way) lovingly take a child with special needs named Lucy*[2] under her wing and protect her from bullying. Later my daughter shared with me that she was so lucky Lucy was her friend. I've reminded myself to "look at that little girl of yours. She gets it! See! You *are* the mother your children need!"

I have used these words on the days I feel like I have failed. On the days the house is a disaster, everything has gone wrong, and I've let the kids eat cereal for dinner because I just haven't been able to face the kitchen, I have said, "It is good for them to see you like this, then get up and try to do better tomorrow. You are teaching resilience, authenticity,

---

2 All asterisks denote name change.

and improvement. You are the mother your children need!"

I have used these words in sorrow. Despite everything we could do, there came a day when I had to face the fact that the little boy I had tried so desperately to adopt would not be coming to our home. He would not, in fact, be my son. My heart was broken. "You don't know why he doesn't get to come home, but you did everything in your power, and no one else has fought as hard as you did for that boy. Even when hard things happen and you don't know how you will get through them, you are still the mother your children need."

You are the mother your children need! These words are my motherhood mantra. I am the mother *my* children need and *you*, dear friend, you are the mother *your* children need.

Each of us has been blessed with God-given gifts, talents, and abilities. Within are the nutrients our children need to grow into the people God means for them to be.

In Moroni 10 and Doctrine and Covenants 46, we are taught about spiritual gifts. Sandwiched between verses twelve and twenty-six in D&C 46 is a list of potential spiritual gifts—each wonderful in its own right. However, reading the first and second verses one after the other in this scriptural block, without the middle verses, is an insightful likening to motherhood's gifts. We read that "to

> There are as many ways to be a good mother as there are mothers in this world who want to be one.

some is given one, and to some is given another, that all may be profited thereby . . . And all these gifts come from God, for the benefit of the children of God."[3] As mothers, our gifts, talents, and abilities are varied. To some, one gift is given, and to some, another gift is given, but all are from God, and all benefit His children. There are as many ways to be a good mother as there are mothers in this world who want to be one.

I was sitting in a publishing meeting in which we were discussing raising children. All present were mothers. There is nothing as cathartic for gathering insight as sitting in a circle with other moms and helping each other become better. As we shared our ideas, I brought up a helpful parenting hack I had recently started using with my family. It was working wonders and spoke to my

---

3 D&C 46:12, 26.

philosophy on life, so I was eager to share it with my friends.

One of my associates whose children are grown spoke up and said, "Wow, I failed my kids. That's not how I did things at all! I wish I had mothered more like you do when my kids were little!"

I was stunned. There in front of me sat a woman who had done a fantastic job raising four children! This was a woman I greatly respected and who took on hard parenting challenges. Had she not been the type of mother she had been, who knows if those children would be the people they are today.

I laughed out loud and said, "But don't you see? You are exactly what your children needed! Look at your kids! They had to have *you* just the way you were."

The way we choose to parent is a composite of our gifts, talents, abilities, and especially our varied life experiences. If only we could see each other's differences as assets to our parenting rather than divisions among us. Our differing political affiliations or parenting philosophies, choices, styles, and routines are assets—not detriments— to our ability to raise amazing children. Elder John K. Karmack said, "May we look for every opportunity, therefore, to decrease isolation, in- crease inclusion of all, and enrich our lives with this diversity of human sociality within the bonds of unifying doctrinal beliefs."[4]

I was a raised by a single mother. Her life circumstance required a different effort from her than was required of most Mormon moms raising children in Utah in the 1980s. My mom was a "yes" mom, whose philosophy was to say yes unless there was a compelling reason to say no. As a result, I got to enjoy having many experiences most kids don't get to have. I had a lot of independence and self-government. Mom believed in and supported my often over-the-top ambitions. She taught me I was limitless! It was the exact parenting I needed to shape me into the person God needed me to be in the world and especially who I needed to be for my own family.

My husband, conversely, was raised by a mother who worked very hard as a stay-at-home mom. She was there for him with milk and cookies upon his arriving home from school. (I still don't measure up to my mother-in-law in the chocolate chip cookie department! And that's okay. I kind of love that my husband and his mother have something that belongs to the two of them.) She was also known school-wide for being the mom who fed a home-made lunch to her son's entire group of rowdy, smelly teenage friends each weekday. Her house was

4 "Unity in Diversity," *Ensign*, March 1991.

immaculately kept and always felt like home. She taught my husband restraint, decorum, peacemaking, hard work, and common sense. These were the exact things my husband needed to prepare him for his purpose in life.

These two mothers were as unalike in mothering styles as they could possibly be, and yet, ultimately, they had more in common than you might think. It is as if they were the bottom two points on a triangle. It doesn't matter how far apart they were; as they made the gospel of Jesus Christ their focus, they met at the top of the triangle. Their love of God, their love of their children, their testimonies of the gospel of Jesus Christ, and their commitment to do all they could to guide their children back to Father are the uniting factors that superseded any difference in style or technique.

All over the world, millions of mothers are parenting children in many varied ways while still pointing their children to Christ. We are the great constellation of mothers united in purpose.

A neighbor and I had the most interesting discussion about our differences. It was one of

> We are the great constellation of mothers united in purpose.

those unexpected conversations that left me alive and full. I had been learning how to clip in to the pedals on my bike by riding around my driveway. When she drove by, she saw my bike upside down, the tire spinning, and me half clipped in to my pedals, spread askew over the concrete. My clipped-in leg was in the air, connected unnaturally to the bike. In what can only be described as an act of mercy, my proficient cyclist neighbor stopped to give me some clipping-in pointers.

After helping me back onto solid ground, our chat turned into deep feelings of the heart, as talks among friends often do. My neighbor said there was a time in her life when she looked at the mothers around her and lamented her deficiencies. She stood in wonder and sometimes, she admitted in humility, judgment . . . especially of the highly scheduled dance moms. How did they do what they did, and why? She saw the experiences they were able to give their daughters and felt that perhaps her own daughters were missing out. But then she said she realized that even though she wasn't a dance mom, she was a pie mom. Her girls might not have pirouetted, but they knew how to make beautiful and delicious pies.

I am not a dance mom, and I am not a pie mom. But I love those moms. I also love the neighborhood doctor moms, beautiful seamstress moms, award-winning baker moms, musician moms, politician moms, entrepreneur moms, soccer moms, and every other kind of mom I know. None of these gifts are mine, but my children have a mom with her own gifts, talents, and abilities—as do your children.

You are the mother your children need. The very one. If they needed to be ballerinas, they would have been sent to the ballerina mom. If they needed to be geographers, they would have been sent to the geography mom. But unless you are a ballerina or a geographer or one who can be highly committed to those things, your children weren't sent for those purposes. They were sent to you for your purpose and theirs.

You: the mom who doesn't know how to do math homework past the third grade but loves to dance in the rain. You: the mom who despises crafting but loves making dinner for her kids. You: the trumpet-playing mom who was never on the drill team but who can relate to your daughter's passion because it is so similar to your own of playing an instrument. You: the mom who can hold your teenager with unparalleled love through the repentance process because you have walked that road before and are better because of it. You: the mom who was once a girl with hopes, dreams, and ambitions essential to shaping her children, skills never meant to be hidden. It doesn't matter where you have been, your life has brought you to this moment. If your hand is in God's hand, you are unstoppable, "for with God nothing shall be impossible."[5]

---

5 Luke 1:37.

Chapter 2
Your Worth, Your Divinity

"His divine power hath given unto us all things that pertain unto life and godliness, through the knowledge of him that hath called us to glory and virtue: Whereby are given unto us exceeding great and precious promises: that by these ye might be partakers of the divine nature."[6]

A friend of mine called me not too long ago to tell me she hadn't received a document I was supposed to have sent her. The truth was I had been sick in bed for weeks and had completely forgotten. Rather than admit the truth, however, I panicked. My friend and I had only recently become acquainted, and I thought if she knew I had forgotten, she would think one of two things: she didn't matter to me, which

---

6 2 Peter 1:3–4.

wasn't true, or I was scatter-brained, which actually *was* true! However, I didn't want her to think either of these things. In essence, I believed that if she saw my imperfection, my worth in her eyes would decrease. And if my worth in her eyes decreased, she must be right. I would be worth *less* because of my mistakes. Worth less equals worthless.

In that moment, I thought, *What am I worth*?

> When we stop looking for ways to prove our worth, we settle into the knowledge of our divinity.

In our Father's eyes, our worth is set. It isn't something we can earn or have taken away. It is infinite and eternal and was purchased for each one of us by a loving Savior. The price tag He put on it was His very life, and He has paid that price no matter our performance. We are of worth simply because we belong to Him.

When we stop looking for ways to prove our worth, we settle into the knowledge of our divinity. Mothers who are aware of their divinity can get to work on the business of teaching their children.

Unfortunately, even when our brains know and accept this concept of worth as logically true, we find it hard to believe. And in not believing our worth, we act in ways that contradict the divine women we are.

Naturally wanting to get as far away from worthlessness as possible and thinking illogically, I grabbed for what I thought was my worth by telling my friend a small lie. I told her that what I was supposed to send her was in the mail rather than admitting I had forgotten. My spur-of-the-moment plan was to run the document to the mail, and no one would be the wiser.

> With my head held low, I finally knelt in prayer and told the story to a God, who already knew it. In sharing my flaws with my Heavenly Father, I turned my pain from unproductive shame to productive Godly sorrow.

Immediately after I hung up, I was full of regret and shame. I put the document in the mail and cried for an hour to myself and then counseled with my husband. With my head held low, I finally knelt in prayer and told the story to a God, who already knew it. In sharing my flaws with my Heavenly Father, I turned my pain from unproductive shame to productive godly sorrow.

In the silence that followed my prayer, He reminded me of the research I had been doing on worth. The way I had reacted wasn't behavior that reflected someone who knew what she was worth. The truth I had discovered in my research of scriptures and modern-day revelation told me my worth would not have diminished if I had admitted my weakness to my friend. My worth wasn't even reduced in the lie I had just told. My worth just *was*. Although wrong and out of character, my behavior had not taken away one ounce of what Christ had paid for me. Christ bought my worth. I was the one who was treating myself like I wasn't worth anything. And I knew what I needed to do.

Restitution was humiliating but in the good and necessary way that comes with growth. It required that I call someone I barely knew and admit I had done wrong. I sat for thirty minutes with the phone in my hand. If she knew me well, I thought, she would know how out of character this was for me. But because we didn't have a long history of shared friendship, she might think I was a serial liar! Ultimately, I had to decide that what I did in this situation reflected what I believed about the Atonement's offer of redemption. I made the call.

> What people think of us is their right and their business, but it cannot influence our worth.

There was never a guarantee that my friend would accept my apology, but that was out of my control. What people think of us is their right and their business, but it cannot influence our worth.

The rest of the story is of little consequence in relation to this concept, but it is enough to say that my friend was gracious. We shared vulnerability, and our friendship deepened. Also of note, the sacrament tasted extra sweet on my lips the next Sunday.

What about you? Are you grabbing for worth? Are you sculpting yourself into something you are not in a vain attempt to hustle for worthiness?

Name-dropping, bragging, self-deprecating, social climbing, comparison, gossip . . . they're all just hustle. The ways we grab for worth are countless but will never bring us what we are looking for. And we do this song-and-dance because we are afraid. "There is no fear in love; but perfect love casteth out fear: because fear hath torment. He that feareth is not made perfect in love."[7]

We're looking for evidence that Christ's love is inside us as a tool to cast away the fear. We are looking for the pieces God made—the unique gifts, talents, and abilities. Sometimes they're hard to see through the posturing and preening we do to prove worthiness, and we don't even need to do any of that. Our worth is already in there. So is our divinity.

The world will strive to siphon your worth into a hole that tells you that you are not enough. Then they'll try to sell you products to "help you" get out of the hole of worthlessness. In reality, their "help" is pushing you back down. No matter how much you hustle, climb, or even buy, you cannot get out of the hole by yourself. An exit can come only with the belief that because of the Savior, you have worth. Enough

7 1 John 4:18.

people have, are, and will tear you down. Don't let yourself be one of them.

Heavenly Father knows everything about us, including our flaws. And yet here we are. We are trusted to raise children, trusted to put their feet firmly on the path back to Him. There are times in my parenting when I wonder, "Why, God? Why would you trust *me* with such a thing?" He trusts me because He knows my worth and He believes in me. In these instances of self-doubt, it would be good for me to "remember the worth of souls is great in the sight of God."[8]

We came from a cocreation between Heavenly Father and Heavenly Mother.[9] As our heavenly parents, They do not question our divinity or worth based on our choices. Knowing our worth, divine nature, *and* flaws, Heavenly Father still allows us to be mothers! Do you believe in your worth and in your divine nature?

Whenever I look at my hands, I see my mom's—long fingers with deep nail beds, the beginning of wrinkles. My hands are not as young as they once were, but I love them because they look just the way I remember Mom's hands when I pressed my palm to hers during sacrament meeting

---

8 D&C 18:10.

9 https://www.lds.org/topics/mother-in-heaven?lang=engm.

as a little girl. I see my hands and feel a kinship to the woman who raised me.

I wonder at the likeness of my hands to my mother's, and it makes me wonder which of my characteristics belong to *Heavenly* Mother? What part of my nature is a reflection of Her? We know we are like our Heavenly Mother—"All men and women are in the similitude of the universal Father and Mother and are literally the sons and daughters of Deity."[10]

My husband taught a lesson to his Primary class that was profound in its simplicity. In trying to teach divine nature to nine-year-olds, he asked if they believed the words they sang in "I Am a Child of God."[11] They nodded their little heads. (Is there anything sweeter than nine-year-olds nodding as they lean forward in their chairs, eager to learn the gospel? No, there is not. They are fresh from baptism, and their little minds are opening up for bigger ideas. They're thirsty for knowledge. If you are called to Primary, beg to teach the nine-year-olds.)

My husband asked them to fill in the blanks to his statements:

10 "The Origin of Man," *Improvement Era*, November 1909, 78.

11 "I am a Child of God," *Children's Songbook*, no. 2.

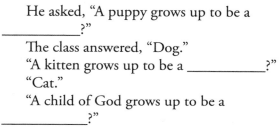

He asked, "A puppy grows up to be a
_____?"

The class answered, "Dog."

"A kitten grows up to be a _____?"

"Cat."

"A child of God grows up to be a
_____?"

Silence. They didn't know if it was okay to say the answer, which was, of course, that a child of God grows up to be a god. It took him several repetitions of this exercise to open their eyes to their divine nature. The Spirit filled the classroom and testified truth as it settled over the minds and hearts of some of the newest members of the Church.

In a statement issued by the First Presidency of the Church in 1909, they stated, in essence, that all children of God can grow up to be a god; thus, a daughter of Heavenly Mother can grow up to be a mother.[12] Whether she bears children or not is immaterial to whether she is the mother her children need. Many of the best mothers I know are stepmothers, godmothers, aunts, and friends who never bore children but, with their divine nature, rear them nonetheless.

12 See "The Origin of Man," *Improvement Era*, November 1909, 78. Reprinted in *Ensign*, February 2002.

These women's lives are not of less import or significance because of the methodology of their mothering.

Not only did God create us to be mothers, but He also instilled within women, regardless of their ability to physically bear children, a deep and instinctual disposition to nurture.

I have a new friend. Her name is Kelly*, and she adopted me after I gave a talk in church. When sacrament meeting ended, I came off the stand to a stranger waiting for me. She was a wheelchair-bound, larger-than-life woman with an oxygen tank, big dimples, a notebook, and a baby doll named Mark* perched under her arm. She didn't introduce herself or the doll, but she declared me her BFF, and that settled it. We speak almost daily. I'm not unique. Kelly has a lot of best friends—her BFFs. If you were one of the lucky ones to meet her, you'd be one too.

Kelly suffered a traumatic brain injury at some time in her life, and while I've heard the story several times with variance in each telling, I don't really know what occurred to compromise Kelly's mind. But I do know God gave Kelly to me and to our ward family to teach us how to love better. In her childlike innocence, she teaches me how to be a better mother. Kelly has a son,

Mark, who is a doll. (Do not call him a doll in front of Kelly though. It infuriates her, and few things match her fury.)

Many of our phone calls are just like any other call I would have with another mom. Our chats are about Mark acting up or Mark cutting a new tooth. I have even heard Mark's birth story! Last month I took a call from Kelly in which she told me Mark was ill and asked if I would please bring them something to help him feel better (a Dr. Pepper half full of ice). I was happy to do that. You see, Kelly does not possess the intellectual ability to be a mother on this earth, yet her heart yearns to mother a child.

On Sundays, I watch Kelly nurture Mark, who is always dressed for the occasion in a suit and tie. (He did wear a large-brimmed baby sombrero to church once.) She feeds him. She burps him. She tells him to shush. And while it can be unconventional and, at times, uncomfortable to watch her parent a doll, I get it. I get her. Motherhood is within all women. It is a divine appointment, part of our very nature.

Sister Sheri L. Dew has said that "motherhood is more than bearing children . . . . It is the essence of who we are as women. It defines our very identity, our divine stature and nature, and the unique traits our Father gave us."[13] And this from a woman who has not born children but who has been mother to many.

What are, as Sister Dew mentioned, the unique traits Father gave you that make you the mother your children need? I don't know what your answer is, but I would bet you carpool duty for a week that the answers to that question are in your patriarchal blessing.

Our patriarchal blessings are like letters from home when we've been away too long. They're warm and full of words of encouragement and love.

I was peeved one Sunday as I stood in the back of a Relief Society room listening to the lesson on patriarchal blessings, bouncing my endlessly colicky second baby. The teacher spoke of how patriarchal blessings reflect who we are. She encouraged us all to use ours as a road map for our lives. She said all the right and true things, yet my peevishness turned to tears as the lesson continued. My exhausted heart didn't know what to feel. It just knew it didn't feel good.

I came home, got the baby to sleep, and sat down to analyze my feelings. I finally realized the mental discord I felt was the belief that I was not the person in my patriarchal blessing. The woman

13 "Are We Not All Mothers?" *Ensign*, November 2001.

and mother described in my blessing was a strong, powerful force for good. I respected her. But it wasn't *me* I was respecting. It was some *her*, a *her* who seemed unattainable.

Our Heavenly Father and our Savior know the end from the beginning. Christ says, "My name is Jehovah, and I know the end from the beginning; therefore my hand shall be over thee."[14] When we receive our patriarchal blessings, we need to keep in mind that our Father gives them to us with the entire picture before Him. He sees us for who we

> When we receive our patriarchal blessings, we need to keep in mind that our Father gives them to us with the entire picture before Him. He sees us for who we were, who we are, and who we can be. The choice to use our agency, to become, is up to us, but our worth, nature, and potential are already set.

---

14 Abraham 2:8.

were, who we are, and who we can be. The choice to use our agency, to become, is up to us, but our worth, nature, and potential are already set.

Begin to believe this, and you will watch with joy as the promises in your blessing come to fruition. These promised gifts, talents, abilities, and experiences will happen for you in their proper time and season. Sometimes you'll even see the same promise in your blessing manifest itself in different ways, depending on your current situation. A promised blessing fulfilled to me in one way in my early twenties has also come to fruition in a completely different way in my late thirties. As I evolve and grow, so do the manifestations of my blessing's promises.

These days I try not to focus on what I'm not in my patriarchal blessing. I try to remember my worth and hold my blessing as a standard for my behavior. I try to remember that patriarchal blessings aren't a promise of some future person but an explanation of a person with gifts within her just waiting to be found.

Go forth in confidence with a knowledge of your divine nature and a belief in your unchangeable worth. Savor the blessings that come from having a testimony of who you are and what you are here for. You are a mother, and you are here to change the world!

Chapter 3
Their Mothers Knew It

There is a moment between day and night when God does His painting. He colors the sky with orange, red, pink, and purple. Sometimes the spirit of the setting sun makes me hold my breath, and all of my questions are answered! (Isn't it amazing how many things resolve themselves when we feel His love?) If we see one of these works of God's sky art while we're driving, I tell the kids to fold their arms but keep their eyes open, fixed on the sunset. I give thanks aloud in prayer. We tell Heavenly Father what we love about His masterpiece: "I love the shape of that one puffy, pink cloud over the temple, Heavenly Father. Thank you!"

Don't worry. You don't have to tell me. I already know this practice is weird, free-spirited, and different. My only excuse is that I was raised by a former member of a rock band who was a devout Mormon hippie.

Elder Brett K. Nattress asked a question that hit home with me: "If all that your children knew of the gospel came from you—as their only source—how much would they know?"[15] It is a daunting thought. There is no parenting responsibility in the world that carries as much weight as the responsibility held in this question.

This past fall, I was watching conference in my favorite one-piece, zip-up-the-front fleece pajamas (that horrify my children) when I heard that statement. I shrank in my chair with the gravity of the words. Understandably, the stress of said statement resulted in my consumption of every last jelly bean in the candy bowl. (We keep candy on the end table during conference as part of a game to keep the kids engaged. Perhaps you know the one—eat a red jelly bean when someone says the word *prayer*. Eat a pink one when someone says the word *fasting*. Eat two when you see Uncle Thomas singing in the choir. *Eat the entire bowl* when the fate of your children's gospel knowledge is put wholly upon your shoulders.)

---

15 "No Greater Joy Than to Know That They Know," *Ensign*, November 2016.

Uh-oh. Uh! Oh! I thought.

I try. Heaven knows I try! I must admit that my children know a whole lot of "I, Nephi, having been born of goodly parents."[16] In fact, they probably have that one memorized. But, please, oh please, do not ask them anything about the Isaiah chapters! They know some stories about their pioneer heritage but probably couldn't give you any sort of reasonable time line of the Restoration.

Do you think praying over sunsets counts as teaching the gospel? I wondered while holding my jelly bean bowl. *If not, this family is in* huge *trouble.*

Just when I was about to have a mommy meltdown, my mantra came to my mind, and I was able to receive the rest of Elder Nattress's lovely talk in peace. I am the mother my children need. So are you. We have what it takes to teach them.

I look over the course of my life and see a pattern. My life, as is the case for all of us on this mortal path, has been a beautiful amalgamation of triumph and trial. There have been moments of intense beauty that I will treasure forever, and there have been experiences of great pain that I have withstood and, even with much work, conquered. It is as clear to me as a reflection on glassy

16 1 Nephi 1:1.

> It is as clear to me as a reflection on glassy water that my never-wavering testimony of God and His Son is what has seen me through from trial to triumph.

water that my never-wavering testimony of God and His Son is what has seen me through from trial to triumph.

Your life and all that *you* have been through fills the well that is your testimony. And that well is exactly what your children need. You love God. You have a testimony of Jesus Christ as your personal Savior. No matter what doubts, questions, or experiences have come your way, you have chosen Him.

Sister, that is enough.

Please don't think I am advocating an abandonment of traditional in-home gospel study in the name of exclusive, free-spirited gospel teaching. We need to attempt a regular pattern of scripture study, family prayer, and all of the other basics in our homes. But life happens to us all, and a pedestal of gospel-teaching perfection will only set our families up for feelings of inadequacy. As long as we are diligently trying to teach the gospel in a way that is consistent with our own family's situation and ability, our children will have what they need in the end because they will see that *we, their mothers, know.*

God does not require us to be perfect scholars of the scriptures or Church historians or to know every answer to every question our children might have. In fact, we are counseled to "trust in the Lord with all thine heart; and lean not unto thine own understanding. In all thy ways acknowledge him, and he shall direct thy paths."[17] We can answer our children's questions, and when we can't, we know where to go for the answers. We know in whom we place our trust. I don't know how to navigate a lot of things, but I trust that God knows. If I am willing, He will show me.

The mothers of the two thousand stripling warriors did not sit idly by in their sons' childhood. They actively taught their sons the gospel. Was it by organized daily lessons, a perfect record of morning scripture study, and never-missed nightly family prayer? We don't know. But somehow I doubt it. Somehow I see more sisterhood with those two thousand warrior mamas whose lives were busy, chaotic, and imperfect as they strived to raise children in an environment of unrest. (Sound familiar?)

How they actually succeeded in raising sons whose valiance made it possible for them to face

17 Proverbs 3:5–6.

battle with such faith will continue to be a mystery to us. The scriptures don't tell us the *how*; they only tell us the stripling warriors "did not doubt their mothers knew it."[18]

And we know the end result: it was faith. The boys didn't just know it for themselves. They knew their mothers knew it too. Their mothers' examples prepared them for the battles they would face.

We give our children the gospel knowledge they need when we show up. We show up in our callings, in service, in love, and in private, when we don't even realize they are watching. Our children are witnesses of our showing up. They see us take meals when someone is sick. When we pull over to help someone on the side of the road, they see that too. They notice when we spend our only free night going to the church in a hideous polyester yellow shirt to help the Webelos. They know "their mothers [know] it."[19]

Paul tells us Timothy's "unfeigned faith" was a direct result of faith "which dwelt first in thy grandmother Lois, and thy mother Eunice."[20] Timothy was as close as a son to the Apostle Paul, and the Bible Dictionary refers to Timothy as Paul's "most trusted and capable assistant."[21]

---

18 Alma 56:48.

19 Ibid.

20 2 Timothy 1:5.

21 Bible Dictionary, "Timothy."

Without the faith of Lois and Eunice, there would not have been a Timothy to assist Paul in furthering the gospel of Jesus Christ. Timothy may not have had the necessary faith to accomplish his potential had it not been for the women before him.

Like Eunice and Lois, we have within us the depth of spiritual capability to provide the foundation our children need. Whoever your children are, they are of utmost importance to our Father in Heaven, and just

> As mothers to our own unique children, our spiritual wells are as deep as God knew they would need to be and are as full as we choose to fill them.

as Timothy, they have a purpose on this earth. With our help, they can become who they are supposed to be in this life. This responsibility isn't anything to fear. As mothers to our own unique children, our spiritual wells are as deep as God knew they would need to be and are as full as we choose to fill them.

What are we putting in our wells? Sunday School answers come to mind: prayer, scriptures, temple attendance. Our experiences in the gospel give us water for our wells. Even our experiences in making mistakes and using the Atonement are vital drops of water added to the well from which our children gain their spiritual foundation.

We quench our children's spiritual thirst when we teach them about the contents of our well while they are in our homes. Teaching the gospel is so much more than a to-do list of scriptures, prayer, and weekly church attendance. Daily gospel practices are of little consequence if our children don't have testimonies of the *why* behind the practice. We are to teach faith in the Lord Jesus Christ, but why? Repentance, but why? Baptism, but why? The laying on of hands for the gift of the Holy Ghost, but why?

The most important item in our well is our personal relationship with Jesus Christ. Practice of a gospel principle without testimony behind the practice will not be enough for our children to withstand the world outside our front doors. Each of our children will learn the gospel and gain their own testimonies differently. Somehow, we have to make our way into their hearts to help them find the why behind what we teach.

Knowing which gospel principles to teach specific to our children's individual needs and knowing

> Practice of a gospel principle without testimony behind the practice will not be enough for our children to withstand the world outside our front doors. Each of our children will learn the gospel and gain their own testimonies differently. Somehow, we have to make our way into their hearts to help them find the why behind what we teach.

the methods that will be most effective in helping them learn comes through personal revelation.

Sister Julie B. Beck gave us what I consider to be a necessary tool of womanhood when she spearheaded the production of the book *Daughters in my Kingdom*. Within its pages is a quote from Sister Beck's April 2010 conference talk. It states, "The ability to qualify for, receive, and act on personal revelation is the single most important skill that can be acquired in this life."[22]

---

22 "And upon the Handmaids in Those Days Will I Pour Out My Spirit," *Ensign*, May 2010.

We are the mothers our children need, and as such, we trust in the Lord. We believe we can receive personal revelation as mothers when we are working to qualify for it. We show Him we are ready for more guidance as we act on the revelation He gives us. When we partner with heaven and show our Father we are serious about needing His help, He will give it.

> When we partner with heaven and show our Father we are serious about needing His help. He will give it.

The world has another term for personal revelation; they call it mother's intuition. This intuition is as simple as a mother's heart being connected to heaven as she receives revelation on behalf of her children.

Revelation for our children doesn't always come right away, but it does come!

My teenager wants a cell phone more than anything in the world. And yet, as her mother, I have not felt it is either right or wrong at this time.

We've been through every argument. The argument, "But, Mom, *everyone* has a phone" wasn't much of a persuasion until I was called to serve in the Young Women program, where I saw how right she was. Everyone but one other girl did, in fact, have a phone. And I know their parents felt it was right at this time.

My husband and I have gone back and forth as we've carefully weighed the decision. On one hand, once she has a phone, it opens a Pandora's box of challenges. On the other hand, as her mother, I have to teach her how to be in the world but not of it. How can I teach her that if I don't allow her into the world at all? She makes good choices. She has presented valid arguments (including the most adorable PowerPoint presentation.) She is responsible.

Back and forth the argument goes as I seek for personal revelation. And yet, the only answer I can give her as I wait for revelation to come is that yes, she can have a phone. . . . I just don't know when.

My daughter has watched me struggle with this. She has heard me pray about it in front of her. She has been a part of conversations and knows there are conversations about it that she isn't privy to. I am teaching her how to seek answer to prayer in my very actions. I am teaching her to wait on the Lord.

We are teaching gospel principles in our homes simply by being ourselves! When crisis comes, may our children see our knees red from kneeling in prayer. When we have an honest doubt or question, let us allow our children to hear it and watch us be seekers as we search for the answer. Let them see where we turn. Where we turn, they will turn.

It is most comforting to remember that I am not alone in teaching my children the gospel. I am not alone in my mothering, for God has promised that angels will walk by my side. To this end, Elder Jeffrey R. Holland, in conjunction with D&C 98:37, says, "I ask everyone within the sound of my voice to take heart, be filled with faith, and remember the Lord has said He 'would fight [our] battles, [our] children's battles, and [the battles of our] children's children.' . . . I testify of angels, both the heavenly and the mortal kind. In doing so I am testifying that God never leaves us alone, never leaves us unaided in the challenges that we face."[23]

I have a giclée print of a painting I love in my home. It is called *She Will Find What Is Lost* by Brian Kershisnik. It is a muted canvas of pale, heavenly greens, blues, and whites. It depicts a woman standing, shoulders slumped with what seems to be the weight of the world pressing down

23 "The Ministry of Angels," *Ensign*, November 2008.

on them. What she is unaware of is the multitude of angelic beings lifting her up. The beings fill the rest of the painting to the top, giving the viewer a sense that the number of people supporting the woman is countless. I like to think of these people as the woman's ancestors, and they carry her in her responsibilities in life.

No, we are not alone in our work, and we are doing well! Elder Holland says,

> May I say to mothers collectively, in the name of the Lord, you are magnificent. You are doing terrifically well. The very fact that you have been given such a responsibility is everlasting evidence of the trust your Father in Heaven has in you. He knows that your giving birth to a child does not immediately propel you into the circle of the omniscient. If you and your husband will strive to love God and live the gospel yourselves; if you will plead for that guidance and comfort of the Holy Spirit promised to the faithful; if you will go to the temple to

both make and claim the promises of the most sacred covenants a woman or man can make in this world; if you will show others, including your children, the same caring, compassionate, forgiving heart you want heaven to show you; if you try your best to be the best parent you can be, you will have done all that a human being can do and all that God expects you to do.[24]

Am I the mother to face the times we live in? Yes. Am I the mother to face the challenges of an online world? Yes. Am I the mother for these children at this time? Yes. Am I the mother to teach my children the gospel principles they need to know? Yes. I am the mother for all these things, and so are you.

The only lasting safety we can offer our children is a knowledge of and commitment to Jesus Christ. With that in mind, I end this chapter in the same way I began—with Elder Nattress's question: "If all that your children knew of the gospel came from you—as their only source—how much would

---

24 "Because She Is a Mother," *Ensign*, May 1997.

they know?" The answer is that they will know as much as you have put in your well . . . a whole lot. You have the spirituality your children need.

> The only lasting safety we can offer our children is a knowledge of and commitment to Jesus Christ.

Chapter 4

Your Children Need the Real You

"Today you are You, that is truer than true. There is no one alive who is Youer than You!" [25]

—Dr. Seuss

Following the birth of my third child, I experienced what I can softly refer to as an identity crisis. My son's birth—my last child—was, shall we say, traumatic. I'll spare you the graphic details that, let's be honest, we mothers love to share . . . . You know we do. In a group of moms, birth stories get more and more intense as everyone contributes to the conversation until pretty soon one woman pushed her child out of her body for seventeen hours uphill both ways IN. A. SNOWSTORM!

---

25 *Happy Birthday to You* (New York City: Random House Children's Books, 1976).

For our purposes, it is enough to say that the complications for many years prior to my son's arrival, his birth itself, and the complications the following week led to my eventual hysterectomy at age thirty-three. So much of my life for the decade prior to this child's birth had been focused solely on motherhood—trying to have children, taking care of them, and trying to have more. I didn't know who I was if I was not the woman bringing children into her home. As I looked to the not-so-distant future, I panicked. I was Mom, the best title of all, but was I anything else? What about the things I used to love to do? Where had they gone, and why? When, in breakdown mode, I finally stopped long enough to notice, I missed so much of who I used to be.

I took some time unpacking the situation and realized I had collected quite the trove of unhelpful and untrue beliefs. Those fallacies had caused me to lose many elements of the person I was. The sketch of who I had been was there, but the drawing seemed to lack color.

When I began my motherhood journey at the youthful age of twenty-three, I had high and unrealistic standards, a long, self-imposed, culturally-though-not-doctrinally influenced list of expectations for myself. I felt that if I were a good mother, I would put myself away, don a 1950s apron, and become June Cleaver. I misinterpreted 1 Corinthians 13:11: "When I was a child, I spake as a child, I understood as a child, I thought as a child: but when I became a [wo]man, I put away childish things."[26]

Put them away I did. The problem was that I put away more than childish things. I put away parts of my essential self. Gone was my involvement in theater, writing, and singing, to name a few. Why on earth did I stop doing the things I loved, and how could I have called it God's will?

As women, we are half of His children. Is it really our belief that His will is to have half of His carefully crafted human beings neglect the talents, gifts, abilities, minds, and ambitions He gave us?

This is not to say we should invest all our time in ourselves. Sacrifice is a beautiful and wonderful thing. It is a daily necessity in motherhood. Sacrifice is how we make sacred our offerings to our Father in Heaven. As Elder Neal A. Maxwell so eloquently said, "The submission of one's will is really the only uniquely personal thing we have to place on God's altar. The many other things we 'give,' brothers and sisters, are actually the things He has already given or loaned to us. However, when you and I finally submit ourselves, by letting our individual wills be swallowed up in God's will, then we are really

---

26 1 Corinthians 13:11.

giving something to Him! It is the only possession which is truly ours to give!"[27] Sacrifice, submission, and selflessness are beautiful, spiritual traits we as mothers can and *should* strive to cultivate. Yet, can we truly cultivate any of these beautiful traits if we are void of the unique gifts, talents, and abilities we were created to have?

It is not the right kind of sacrifice to give up on ourselves and say with a martyr's sigh that it is for our families. Showing our children that Mom doesn't matter is not the right and selfless thing to do. In Psalms, David says we are "fearfully and wonderfully made"[28] by God! He did not make us to ask us to turn our backs on everything that makes us unique just because we become mothers. His desire for us is to learn balance.

In order to see what I'd lost, I began to investigate what pieces I felt I was missing and how I could get them back. I knew putting things back the way they had been would never work. There were some things that just wouldn't fit me anymore, and that was okay. That was growth.

It was a process to discern which of the things I enjoyed were "hobbies" and which were divine

---

27 "Swallowed up in the Will of the Father," *Ensign*, November 1995.

28 Psalms 139:14.

characteristics. For example, I discovered that knitting was more of a hobby for me. It was fun, but it didn't awake any sort of spiritual connection inside me. (The truth of the matter is that I let my sister-in-law rope me into a visit to the craft store, where I had a glorious time spending forty dollars on yarn to make one dishrag that I never finished. Conversely, for my sister-in-law, knitting is part of her divine self that I hope she never lets slip away in the busyness of life. When I see the half-done dishrag I knitted, I see fun. When I see the beautiful sweaters, mittens, scarves, blankets, and booties my sister-in-law creates, I see part of who she was before she came to this earth! I learned that what may be a simple hobby for one may be part of another person's divine identity. But I digress.)

After discerning what was divine for my own self, I took every lost piece I felt was a part of that divine self and put it back on the table. Before absorbing it all back in though, I ran it through a sieve of prayer, thought, counsel with my husband, and the constraints of my life. Some things slipped right through the sieve and were gone for good . . . happy to live in the memories of my past. There were other aspects of me I definitely wanted to put back but couldn't work in within the time and season of my life. I put those away

. . . but not forever, just for a later time. What remained had to come back as soon as possible, even if I didn't know how it would happen.

One of the things I missed desperately was performing. Some might consider performing a hobby, but for me, it is part of who I am. I have performed professionally since the age of three. Acting wasn't something I had to work on much in my youth; it was a gift I was born with and enjoyed until I was married, until some negative experiences led me to believe (rightly or wrongly) I couldn't be a value-driven mom and an actor, so I cut it out of my life without thought of the consequence.

After determining this was a part of me that needed to be restored, I was at a loss as to how to incorporate it back into my life. In the past, people had sought after my talents, and I had enjoyed a thriving career in the performing arts, but that life felt so far away. I was a decade removed from my contacts and hadn't sung a note publicly in years. I began looking at audition notices and decided to follow through on several, only to back out at the last second—afraid that all my talent had shriveled up and died.

Keeping prayer as a part of the process, I told Heavenly Father I wanted to be involved in performing again but I was scared. I was going to need

His help to make me brave. Around this time, my
stake was putting on a play. I hadn't been asked to
participate in the play, but one Sunday, a member
of the stake Relief Society presidency sat in front of
me. At the end of the meeting, she turned to me
and complimented me on my voice. I uncomfort-
ably expressed my gratitude for her kind words,
and we went our separate ways. That night, she
called and said she felt strongly that I was supposed
to be in the play. I believe this was a direct answer
to my prayer. Heavenly Father knew I wouldn't say
no to this sister, so He'd prompted her to ask me
to participate.

I played no role of significance. I was a highly
trained actress with scores of professional credits, yet
I had one line (it was, "We must go west!" in case
you care to know). One line, and it was an amazing
experience for which I was so grateful!

From there, I decided to audition for a community play. A good friend was directing it, and
it felt less scary to return when I knew my "judge"
loved me. I did well in the audition, but the callback was horrific. No, really. It was horrible. I
stopped singing in the middle of the callback and
said, "I just can't do this," and sat down. It ended
with me covered in a mess of snotty tears in my
car. I include this as part of the story because it is
important. When seeking to restore the gifts we

have neglected, we have to be willing to fail. And fail we will.

My friend cast me in the ensemble of the show with my two daughters, whom I'd taken with me to the audition. And the three of us had an amazing time.

One night as we drove home from the theater, my daughter said, "Mom, I like you at the play! You are so fun!" When I asked her what she meant, she explained that she and her sister saw me differently when we were at the theater. They saw me shine, they saw me fulfilling part of the measure of my creation, and I did it with them by my side. I wasn't just the nag of the house. I was bright, funny, and full of life. I was so glad they saw me like this because not too long from now, they too will be mothers. And I want to see them shine.

I want to see my daughter Hailey engaged in science projects at her kitchen counter with her kids. I want to see Libby, my younger daughter, teaching dance lessons in a studio where her own daughters are learning to dance. I invest so much of myself in these tiny people. It would be a shame for them to neglect their gifts. It's imperative that I show them how to keep their divine selves alive . . . even when they are mothers. And the best way I know how to do that is to see my own talents, gifts, and abilities as divine and necessary.

Fast forward five years, and I am once again a professional actor. I am asked to perform on stage regularly. If answers to prayer and consideration of our family's circumstances permit, I accept with joyful delight, often with my children performing at my side.

Each night when I'm done performing, I stand backstage, staring at the empty theater. I breathe in the smell of dust and paint. I close my eyes and hear the echoes of the audience's laughter lingering over the empty seats. I offer a prayer of thanks to have this part of me restored. A great irony of life is how easy it is to be grateful to have something you thought you had lost.

> How easy it is to be grateful to have something you thought you had lost.

I wish I had shown my children who I am all along. How I wish I had taken my kids to the theater with me earlier. I may never perform on a Broadway stage, but I cannot imagine more joy than I experience when sharing the stage with my children.

God made you love what you love for a reason. And He adores you. Sometimes I wish He
had created me to love curing cancer, but I cannot deny the beauty of making someone laugh
while I perform. It makes my insides flip with
happiness. And maybe the person who laughed
at my performance was a doctor. Maybe she is in
the middle of finding a cure for cancer and my
role was to lighten her burden. We are all in this
thing together, and we can't place value on our
gifts as better than or less than anyone else's gifts.

I grew up in a ward with Sister Julie B. Beck,
who asked me to accompany her when speaking
at firesides in our area. I loved my time with her,
and what an honor it was to learn from her. In
2007, I wrote her a letter to which she replied.
She hoped I was still acting (I was not), saying my
children needed my abilities. She told me about
her daughter Geri, who had been a geographer
prior to having children. Geri's walls of her home
were now covered in maps, and she was teaching her children what she knew. "Mothers who
know, teach their children what they know" was
her message to me.

What are the unique things about you that
make you just the right mother for your children?
What are the things about you that your children

need that no one else can offer? Because of your gifts, talents, and abilities, what are the things your children get to experience in your home?

Gifts, talents, and abilities are frequently seen as synonyms. While they most certainly can be interchangeable terms, they are notably different.

Our gifts are features given to us without our earning them or working for them. Our Father gives them to us for the purpose of building up His kingdom but also because He loves and delights in us. Our talents are the aspects of our lives we thrive in, are drawn to, and/or naturally excel in. Talents are similar to gifts but are developed and improved with hard work. Our abilities are the things we have power to do within the circumstances of our lives.

Often we see gifts, talents, and abilities as external—a beautiful singing voice, athletic ability, artistic capabilities, etc.—but I would challenge us to look deeper and not discount the spiritual gifts, talents, and abilities most essential in raising our children.

Don't be afraid of what others think of what parts of you you choose to develop. If you know that being a reader is essential, you need to read. One of my sisters-in-law is an avid reader. She never let that part of herself go, devouring several books a week. She enjoyed mostly fiction. Some might think it not of worth for someone to read that much fiction . . . especially when the reader is a mother to little children. "Wasn't there something more valuable she could do with her time?" many wondered. No. There wasn't. It was part of her divine self. This sister of mine went on to parent two children who have learning challenges. Because they have a mother who is so well-read and articulate, they got what they needed. They got a mother who knows how to verbally advocate for her children and how to help them with their learning challenges. Her two children have ended up being very successful students, and now that they are older, my sister works at a school where she helps children every day. What if she had stopped reading when she was a young mother, as so many in our culture encouraged her to do?

However you choose to be you, just don't put yourself away on a dusty shelf. Putting who you are on the shelf deprives your children of really knowing you.

Determining what we do with our time and what to put into our lives is not an easy business. It isn't a process we do once and never need to do again. It is, rather, a constant evaluation, and we may find that the gifts, talents, and abilities we are compelled to include in our lives may change based on our personal growth. Depending upon the times and seasons in our lives, we may let go of some and be excited to incorporate new ones.

Participating in theater looks much different for a mother with small children than it does for a mother with children who are all grown. A writer with a baby may write by dictating voice notes into her phone's voice recorder while breastfeeding, while a writer with teenagers might take her son with her on a week-long writing retreat. The important thing is that they are both writing. A CPA with a kindergartener may teach her children the love of numbers and reasoning with games around the kitchen table and take clients only during tax season, while a CPA with adult children may work full-time, lapping up the joy of helping people with their financial matters year round.

This is not an exact science. Numerous times I have filled my life with something wonderful but have had to take it off of my plate again in the name of balance. You may experience some trial and error. In the ebb and flow of family life, it is necessary to continually evaluate and find that "just right" place of balance—just right for you and for your family. But never is it necessary to give up completely on your gifts, talents, and abilities.

As we invite our children to join us and immerse them in our life's work, we inspire them to dare to have dreams for their own lives. My neighbor, a politician, canvasses the neighborhood, distributing political information with her children in tow. The entire family is politically active and civically minded. Another friend is a dancer who teaches with her baby strapped to her chest. While my children may never pursue theater, my neighbor's children may never be politicians, and my friend's children may choose a different sport over dance, the lessons our children learn by our sides will apply to whatever they choose to become.

> In the ebb and flow of family life, it is necessary to continually evaluate and find that "just right" place of balance—just right for you and for your family. But never is it necessary to give up completely on your gifts, talents, and abilities.

In no way am I suggesting that we put too much on our plates or that we burden our lives. Nor am I suggesting that we engage in activities that take us away from our children more than is appropriate as determined through personal revelation. My encouragement is to do what you love *with* those you love.

Leaders, from Sister Belle Spafford, Relief Society general president and fierce defender of human rights for women, to Elder Dallin H. Oaks, Apostle, to Sister Beck, Relief Society general president, have encouraged us to be very careful about what we put on our plates.

They have said:

"The average woman today, I believe, would do well to appraise her interests, evaluate the activities in which

> As we invite our children to join us and immerse them in our life's work, we inspire them to dare to have dreams for their own lives.

she is engaged, and then take steps to simplify her life, putting things of first importance first, placing emphasis where the rewards will be greatest and most enduring, and ridding herself of the less rewarding activities."[29]

29 Belle S. Spafford, *A Woman's Reach* (Salt Lake City: Deseret Book, 1974), 23.

"Most of us have more things expected of us than we can possibly do."[30]

"Mothers who know do less."[31]

This is not an issue of doing more; it is a question of what we are doing when we have the time and an encouragement to be authentic in how we choose to fill our time.

For years, I was on the PTA board. I love the PTA and what it does for my children. However, it was not my gift, and I found myself feeling resentful of the time I spent there, then feeling guilty for feeling resentful! Let me be clear, I am so thankful I have dear friends whose gift it is to serve on the PTA. My children come home regularly with joyous stories about experiences they've had at school because of the PTA. But my participation on the board, because I thought it was something I was supposed to do to be a good mom, wasn't the proper use of my time. As I became more authentically myself, I stepped aside from the role, allowing someone else to fill it.

When we step aside from the things we are not passionate about, we make room for those who *are* passionate to take the reins and fulfill their purpose. When I resigned from the PTA, I was able to shift my focus to Peer Parenting, a state-sponsored program

30 Dallin H. Oaks, "Good, Better, Best," *Ensign*, November 2007.

31 Julie B. Beck, "Mothers Who Know," *Ensign*, November 2007.

that teaches parenting skills to mothers who are in danger of having their children removed from their homes. I came alive working with those mothers.

The Peer Parenting program is not more important than the PTA program. They are both necessary. I wasn't switching a bad thing for a good thing. I was switching a "wrong thing for me" to a "right thing for me." Stop doing what you think you *should* be doing, and start doing what you were created to do. As we embrace rather than shun the things we are drawn to or are gifted in, we become authentically ourselves and are able to more clearly define our path forward in motherhood and life.

Authenticity is becoming a virtue increasingly difficult to cultivate. As face-to-face interaction becomes rarer and social-media interaction becomes the norm, it is difficult to discern what is real and what is not. Allowing ourselves to be seen is a scary business, but no one relates to perfection. When you are real, you are relatable and you can change lives. Be cautious what you post on social media. There is a fine line between creating a caricature of perfection and sharing too much information. Be mindful that your children will someday see the electronic trail you left. Is the person represented on your online presence the real you?

Regarding you: You may prepare nutritious meals for your family, but you are not *just* a cook.

You may clean the house, but you are not *just* a housekeeper. You may drive seven carpools, but you are not *just* a chauffeur. Those are things you do out of love, and they can be enjoyable, but what you really are is a wonderfully made daughter of God. You were made to do all that motherhood requires, but perhaps He made you to *also* be a chef, a pianist, a lawyer, a performer, a salesperson, an artist, a reader, a speaker, or a historian. Don't let her go. Choose to be her. You will inspire your daughters to choose to be themselves. You will inspire your sons to be with and support women who are themselves. Your children will know you, and there is power there.

What if Eliza R. Snow had not been a poet? Belle Spafford had not been a defender of women's rights? The mothers of the 2,000 stripling warriors had not been gospel testators? Lucy Mack Smith had not been a writer? Minerva Teichert had not been an artist? Susan Easton Black had not been a historian? Chieko Okazaki had not been an elementary school principal? Our world, the scriptures, and our neighborhoods are full of amazing women—including mothers—whose gifts, talents, and abilities have the power to change the world . . . starting with their very own children. Whoever you are, we need you!

Who is the real you, and what is she missing in her life? Remember, you did—you do—have

dreams, goals, gifts, abilities, talents, and ambitions. You did not arbitrarily think up those things;
our all-knowing Heavenly Father gave them to you
to be used for specific purposes. Whoever you are,
find her today! The world is missing you and so are
your children.

> Remember, you did — you do — have dreams, goals, gifts, abilities, talents, and ambitions. You did not arbitrarily think up those things; our all-knowing Heavenly Father gave them to you to be used for specific purposes. Whoever you are, find her today! The world is missing you and so are your children.

Chapter 5
Creating and Living Your Family's Story

Does it ever seem to you that once we become mothers, it is as if our lives are determined by our children's schedule? Our first child is born, and soon we find our time is spent going from one nap to the other, from one doctor's appointment to the next. Have you ever felt as if life is just happening to you? What if instead of your life happening to you, *you happen to your life*? In 2 Nephi 2:26, we read in part: "They have become free forever, knowing good from evil; *to act for themselves and not to be acted upon*."[32] Most of the time when we read this phrase that appears numerous times in scripture and is popular in our culture, we are most likely thinking about our agency as the right to choose between good and evil. And yet *agency* is a term that extends far beyond choices between right and wrong.

32 2 Nephi 2:26; emphasis added.

The invitation to act rather than be acted upon is more than just a command to choose to be good. It is an invitation to choose the life you want to have, to choose your reactions to the experiences you encounter on your path, to choose what you put on and take off of your motherhood plate. We are agents of our own lives . . . and, to some extent, our children's lives. This is one of the weightiest responsibilities we as mothers have in this life. I adore the words of J.R.R. Tolkien: "All we have to decide is what to do with the time that is given us."[33]

Look at your family's life as a story. You and God are the authors. What are you writing? Does your to-do list hold the pen to the paper of your life, or do you?

In order to *happen* to our

---

33 *The Fellowship of the Ring*, copyright 1954.

own lives, I have found the following four practices extremely helpful: Being intentional with our family stories. Creating moments that matter. Changing our perspective from mundane to meaningful. Allowing the Savior to rewrite the story.

Being Intentional with Our Family Stories

Each night before my children go to bed, I snuggle up to them in their respective rooms. I lay close enough to smell their hair and ask, "Is there anything you want to talk to me about?" Everything about their day seems to slip out so comfortably in a few one-on-one moments. We solve the problems in their worlds within those sacred seconds. These minutes, while powerful, don't just happen to us. They are intentional, meaning that I have to choose to take the minutes away from something else to give them to my children.

It is hard to be intentional when we don't have a clear vision of where we are headed.

As members of The Church of Jesus Christ of Latter-day Saints, we have testimonies as to what can happen in the end. We want to live in such a way that we qualify to live with our families forever in the company of our Heavenly Parents and Jesus Christ. Thus "the end" becomes "the beginning."

In addition to this eternal end, what else do you want?

My sister-in-law Erin and I were talking about this during one of our phone chats one day. Her child was throwing chicken nuggets at her, and mine was on the potty, but it didn't matter. Some of life's best conversations happen while wiping tiny bottoms. In that conversation, Erin and I decided we know exactly what we want at the end of our lives: we want Uncle Merrill's funeral.

My great-uncle Merrill Wilson and his wife, Aunt LaRae, were these odd, wonderful, intentional parents. They didn't do things like other families did. Uncle Merrill and Aunt LaRae had been raised on farms in the Teton Valley; however, Uncle Merrill had passed up the country, opting instead to become a prominent surgeon in a big city. Nevertheless, they wanted their children to learn the ethics of farm life. So they built a farm, right in the middle of downtown Salt Lake City! It was a farm complete with chickens, sheep, geese, and a highly impressive state-fair-winning fruit-and-vegetable garden. In addition, each child was musically gifted and played instruments, and the entire family sang together. Their house was heated by giant ceramic stoves called Kachelofens and was cooled with irrigation water running through pipes in their house.

It was a strange and special upbringing for their nine children and others too. Their home was open to more than their nuclear family. They laid out large Sunday dinner spreads each week. The widows, the poor, and the city dignitaries sat across the table from one another and broke bread. And the Wilson door was open wide to two impish little children whose mother could never have raised them alone through those lean, single-mother years. That single mother was my mom. And the rascally children were my brother and me.

At Uncle Merrill's funeral, an entire chapel was filled to the brim with the progeny of Uncle Merrill and Aunt LaRae. They sang, and they told stories about their oddly wonderful, larger-than-life upbringing. They bore testimony. This powerful couple had raised a family intentionally according to what was important to them: God, family, work, music, service, farming, and fun.

The Spirit at the service was palpable and comfortable and made me long to be a child again . . . lying under the grand piano while Aunt LaRae played. As I sang in the funeral choir (singing an obscure and impossible-to-sing choral piece Uncle Merrill had selected, of course) I looked out at the congregation and saw clearly the effects Uncle Merrill and Aunt LaRae's intentionally created family story had on hundreds of people.

To be intentional, we have to conscientiously take the time to discern what is meant for our lives, then live to that end. I'm sure farming in the middle of a metropolis wasn't easy for my aunt and uncle. It didn't just happen. They had to *build* what was important to them.

I want Uncle Merrill's funeral! At the end of my days on this earth, I want my family gathered together in celebration of the way I created my own unique family. I may not ever own geese or raise chickens—and I don't want to—but our family's life will likewise have been weirdly and intentionally created in our own way.

My children will remember eating nachos after church every Sunday.

I hope they'll sing Billy Joel's "Good night My Angel" to their babies at night because I sang it to them.

Perhaps they'll have the patience to endure their own children's events because they'll be able to clearly picture the entire family cheering at swim meets, band competitions, track meets, plays, dance performances, choir concerts, and sporting events.

Maybe they'll take to the mountains where they will transcend this world and sing John Denver songs with their arms reaching through the aspens and into the sky.

My prayer is that when things are hard, they'll remember to rely on the memories of a childhood home that depended on the Savior.

This is what we are trying to do. It is one of millions of right ways to happen to our own lives.

What is your right way? Whatever your family does, do it on purpose! Be intentional.

Creating Moments That Matter

What good are intentions if they never materialize? We act on our lives when we choose to create the intentional life we have so carefully planned in our minds.

My daughter Hailey's birthday caught me off guard one year. I don't know how it happened, as, interestingly enough, her birthday tends to come on the thirteenth of June every single year. My only defense is that this particular year, that was an unusually busy week. We planned on a bigger family celebration on the weekend due to our schedule, so her birthday itself was, to put it bluntly, dead on arrival. There were a couple of gifts on the table, purchased at the last minute and not very thoughtfully selected. They were wrapped in baby-shower wrapping paper because we were out of birthday paper. The decorations didn't exactly scream "Happy Birthday!" either.

Our house, usually decorated on birthdays with multicolored crepe paper and balloons, sat mostly empty, save a hastily tied bow of crepe paper remnants and a solitary pink balloon that was leaking its air and drooping.

"It's okay, Mom. I understand" was how she started the day. She accepted her gifts with kindness and gratitude but perhaps a little confusion at the randomness. ("Gee, Mom, I've always wanted a . . . spatula?" Yes, one of the gifts was a spatula. I am not proud of this fact.) I encouraged her to "hurry and open them; we have to go."

Her dad had a meeting that day, and she, her sister, and I had a dress rehearsal for a play. It was summer, so there were no school celebrations, and in the spare moments we did have, she couldn't find a single friend home to come over and play with her. I told you, it wasn't a great birthday.

As we were driving home that night, I looked in the rearview mirror and saw her face slumped into her hand, the side of her head pressed up against the window. Her eyes were sad and a little wet, though not yet leaking tears. I could see that those beautiful brown eyes were looking at me and saying, "Thank heaven, it's almost over." I tried to make myself feel better by reminding myself that we would celebrate on the weekend, but I saw her face, and I just knew; the weekend wasn't today—today was her birthday, and she thought no one cared.

I felt like a failure as a mother. With sadness sneaking into my heart via the pitiful view from the rearview mirror, I remembered the birthdays of my youth. My mom made such a big deal of them. When I thought about what I treasured about those birthdays, I realized it wasn't the grandeur of how my mother celebrated. It was the way she made me feel completely loved that made the difference.

One of my favorite poets, Maya Angelou, often borrowed a quote from Carl W. Buehner, a General Authority in the Church in the late 1950s and early 1960s. The quote reads, "They may forget what you said, but they will never forget how you made them feel."[34]

Immediately, I went into fix-it-mom mode. It was 10:30 p.m. No time for an impromptu party, but there was still time for us to create a beautiful story. My eyes darted around, and my brain buzzed. What could we do? What could we do? What could we do? Then I saw it.

We were approaching a park that had its sprinklers on. They were the high-pressure sprinklers

---

34 http://quoteinvestigator.com/2014/04/06/they-feel/.

that spray water in a jerking motion to one side, then back to the other side in one long spray. Chik-chik, chik-chik, Chhhhhhhhhhh. I pulled up to the park, turned the car off, and started to take my shoes off. When the kids looked at me with that familiar "Mom is a maniac" face, I told them to do the same. "Take your shoes and socks off," I said.

"What are we doing?" they asked.

"Celebrating Hailey's birthday, of course!" I replied as if this were the plan all along.

Immediately, that sullen face in the backseat lit up.

They shed their shoes, and the three of us ran through the sprinklers in the dead of night, the stars our only witnesses. We splashed and went down slides and sang "Happy Birthday" to Hailey in opera voices. Up and down the field we ran, three sopping-wet, barefoot, crazy people, screaming things like, "We love Hailey," and "Hailey is the birthday princess." We laughed till our bellies ached. A police car started circling the park, adding a touch of excitement. The girls were convinced we were about to be hauled off to jail. In nervous delight, we bolted to the car and got in, collapsing onto our seats in heaps of sagging clothes and giggles, with grass clippings covering our wet bodies. Shivering with the intoxicating feeling of being alive, we drove home.

Whenever anyone says the word *birthday*, Hailey brings up this story. She can perfectly relay how she was sure she was going to be arrested for trespassing. I love her laugh as she tells people, "My mother is crazy." I've heard her tell the story countless times, and whenever she retells it, it ends with, "That was the best birthday."

What easily could have been a horror story of her worst birthday ever, instead became a story she will tell her children with fondness. And the truth of the matter is it hinged on one magical moment. Creating it was free, fast, and easy, yet intentional.

When the time came, I knew what I needed to do to fix the situation. I knew how to create the moment. When we as mothers live our stories in companionship with the Holy Ghost, what we

> When we as mothers live our stories in companionship with the Holy Ghost, what we need to do and say will be given to us "in the very hour, yea, in the very moment" we need it.

need to do and say will be given to us "in the very hour, yea, in the very moment"[35] we need it.

Any day can be extraordinarily created. I always love it when the Apostles back me up. President Dieter F. Uchtdorf says,

> If you are a mother, you participate with God in His work of creation—not only by providing physical bodies for your children but also by teaching and nurturing them. . . .
>
> You may think you don't have talents, but that is a false assumption, for we all have talents and gifts, every one of us. The bounds of creativity extend far beyond the limits of a canvas or a sheet of paper and do not require a brush, a pen, or the keys of a piano. Creation means bringing into existence something that did not exist before—colorful gardens, harmonious homes, family memories, flowing laughter. . . .

---

35 D&C 100:6.

> The more you trust and rely
> upon the Spirit, the greater your
> capacity to create. That is your
> opportunity in this life and your
> destiny in the life to come. Sis-
> ters, trust and rely on the Spirit.
> As you take the normal oppor-
> tunities of your daily life and
> create something of beauty and
> helpfulness, you improve not
> only the world around you but
> also the world within you.[36]

The study of creation is fascinating. I love that President Uchtdorf reminds us that as we create, we improve the world around us, includ-ing ourselves. So let us create the lives we want to live with the people we love, recognizing that creation looks different at every age and stage of life. The life I create with my babies is going to be different from the life I create with my teen-agers.

My mother was still raising my youngest brother, Morgan, when I was raising my own chil-dren. I once pointed out what a different mother Mom was to me than to my younger siblings, and

36 "Happiness, Your Heritage," *Ensign*, November 2008.

> Creation is a living process, evolving as our families grow. As our lives and circumstances change, our abilities to be the mother our children need will also shift.

she retorted with, "You got my youth, and Morgan got my wisdom." It was a wise comment in itself, and she now frequently reminds me of it. I was feisty and strong-willed. I needed her youthful energy. Morgan is tender and more internal. He needed her tender wisdom.

Creation is a living process, evolving as our families grow. As our lives and circumstances change, our abilities to be the mother our children need will also shift.

Changing Our Perspective: From Mundane to Meaningful

Are you energized and excited about being an intentional creator of your family's story? Me too! I hate to be the wet blanket, but I have one word that might kill your buzz. Insert foreboding music and thunder claps. The word is . . . *laundry*. Dun, dun, dun. It is great to have beautiful, well-thought-out plans for a life of intentional, creative story living, but then comes reality.

Laundry, carpools, cleaning up spilled milk (Again? For real? After five spills at one meal, it actually does feel worth crying over.), and let's face it . . . nagging. (Do your kids think you like nagging? My kids think it's my favorite thing. I despise nagging. Do you know how many times I have begged my children not to make me nag them?) The monotony of everyday, mundane mothering tasks threatens to pull us away from our intentionally created stories and back into the place of being acted upon. (FYI: As I am writing, an entire sink of dishes has acted upon me. Does it really take seven dishes to make one cup of hot chocolate? *Seven*!?!) How do you live your story when you have loads and loads of laundry to do?

Many Sundays ago in church, a woman who (side note: was wearing a bonnet so adorable it made me think we should all be wearing bonnets to church) said she prints out pictures of Jesus and put them everywhere there's a monotonous task to be done. The pictures are to remind her that everything she does as a mother is for Him. I absolutely loved her sentiment. I didn't go home and print out pictures of Christ, but I did become mindful of the mundane things I do each day. The next time I stood at the washing machine and every other time I have done a load of laundry since, I have repeated to myself, "There's one more sock for Jesus!"

Yes, the first time I said it, I burst out laughing, but as silly as it sounds, I felt better. I was washing the filthy, grass-stained socks of God's precious little ones. The children who mean so much to Him that He was willing to send our Savior to die for them. Did Christ Himself not say throughout the New Testament, "Suffer the little children to come unto me?" And my goodness, the laundry never ends, but I love God's/my children.

When we change our perspective, even the mundane can have meaning, and meaning is story.

> When we change our perspective, even the mundane can have meaning, and meaning is story.

I have a sign hanging in my living room that says, "Life is

made of moments." It's miserable to scrub the unders of a potty-training toddler, but it is an honor when I think of that little boy as a potential god. It is rough to endure hours upon hours of carpooling to dance but awesome to watch a recital and think that I contributed to developing the talents God instilled in my child. It is bone-tired exhausting to look at a pile of bills but joyful to work to care for His little ones. The magic is in changing the way we look at our responsibilities.

Even when we change perspective, there is a lot of in-between time sandwiched in the midst of moments of pure wonder that we get to experience with our children. Yet I would gladly live an entire week of working hard to attach meaning to monotony if I knew at the end of the week I would have a Hailey-in-the-sprinklers-on-her-birthday moment. It is easy to live life to the fullest in the obvious magical moments, like religious ceremonies and when our children have achievements, but isn't most of what we get in motherhood the moments of normal? Those normal moments are the times in which we get to create. They are where miracles happen.

The goal is not one-hundred percent meaningful, life-changing, story-writing moments. The goal is to shift perspective so that when the sprinkler moments come, we are able to be wholly present. And as we are able to be fully, gratefully present, the moments will increase. There is magic to be found every day. Have patience with yourself as you find it. And when you do, let the monotony go and soak the magic in. Etch it into the cells and neuron groups in your brain whose job it is to store memories for the eternities.

> Let the monotony go and soak the magic in. Etch it into the cells and neuron groups in your brain whose job it is to store memories for the eternities.

Allowing the Savior to Rewrite the Story

President Uchtdorf has said, "How grateful I am to my Heavenly Father that in His plan there are no true endings, only everlasting beginnings."[37]

There is no story so tragic it is not able to be rewritten by the power of our Savior's Atonement.

37 "Grateful in Any Circumstances," *Ensign*, May 2014.

The Savior is the great editor and can come through with a delete key big enough to backspace any mistake. With unconditional love and complete understand-

> With unconditional love and complete understanding, Christ rewrites the stories of the world with redemption!

ing, Christ rewrites the stories of the world with redemption! He does this because the story of the world says that if we make a mistake in our parenting, no amount of repentance is enough. "Not so!" says Christ as He forgives and teaches us how to be better mothers. The world would tell us to let our children go when their choices differ from ours, but with the Atonement, the conclusion of this story can be one of love. He can even rewrite the story of the world that insists the death of a child is the end. His Love shows us instead that death itself is not the end but is a soul-wrenching beginning to a new chapter of a story. And in His version, we hold our baby again!

* * *

I know firsthand that at the end of the day, it is sometimes hard to see the end from the beginning, but I am encouraged by Elder David A. Bednar's view on living and creating our family story:

> In my office is a beautiful painting of a wheat field. The painting is a vast collection of individual brushstrokes—none of which in isolation is very interesting or impressive. In fact, if you stand close to the canvas, all you can see is a mass of seemingly unrelated and unattractive streaks of yellow and gold and brown paint. However, as you gradually move away from the canvas, all of the individual brushstrokes combine together and produce a magnificent landscape of a wheat field. Many ordinary, individual brushstrokes work together to create a captivating and beautiful painting.
>
> Each family prayer, each episode of family scripture study, and each family home evening is a

> brushstroke on the canvas of our
> souls. No one event may appear to
> be very impressive or memorable.
> But just as the yellow and gold
> and brown strokes of paint com-
> plement each other and produce
> an impressive masterpiece, so our
> consistency in doing seemingly
> small things can lead to significant
> spiritual results."[38]

We must have faith that as the mothers our children need, we can be intentional livers and creators of our family's stories. When we are willing to change our perspectives and are eager to allow the Savior to edit our stories when necessary, we are painting stunning wheat fields. We are writing stories for the ages, and when our children leave our homes, they will look back on their time with us with pleasure and perhaps even gratitude.

My sweet son asked me the other day, "Mommy, if you die, will you take your laptop to heaven?"

"No, sweet boy," I said. "We don't take any 'thing' to heaven."

"Then what *do* we take, Mom?" he asked.

---

38 David A. Bednar, "More Diligent and Concerned at Home," *Ensign*, November 2009.

My reply to him was this: "At the end of our lives, when all is said and done, we take what is in our heart and what is in our mind. I will take all the memories we have created, all the things I have learned, my testimony, and the love I have for other people. That's it."

We live intentionally created lives to have memories for our children to take with them to build their own lives. But our children aren't the only ones for whom we create. We create for ourselves as well.

My daughter Elisabeth will never remember splashing in the surf of the Oregon coast in galoshes when she was three years old, her blonde curls framing her face and her voice so tiny in the hiss of the waves' mist. But *I* will remember her that way. When our children are grown and gone, leaving us with empty rooms and the reprieve from laundry we crave, we will be left with only the memories we have so purposefully created in our mothering lives. Left alone, we will retrieve those memories from our hearts as if from a treasure chest. One by one, we'll examine and relive them, full of awe and gratitude at a life well-lived, before softly replacing them in our heart-box to be enjoyed another day.

When our children are grown and gone, leaving us with empty rooms and the reprieve from laundry we crave, we will be left with only the memories we have so purposefully created in our mothering lives.

Chapter 6

Caring for Your Body, Mind, and Spirit

Remember when you used to shave your armpits? Yeah, so do I. Those were the days, right? It seems like there is very little time to care for ourselves in this marathon called motherhood. We are rolling out of bed early and rolling back into bed late. We have feedings, doctor appointments, three carpools, parent-teacher conferences, Church responsibilities, laundry, food preparation, and professional endeavors—the list never ends. The thought of our own wants and needs sometimes seems almost laughable. However, I do not believe that living a life of self-depletion is what Heavenly Father wants for His daughters.

President Gordon B. Hinckley gave us a peek into the aspects Heavenly Father would have us, His daughters, care for. "Of all the creations of the Almighty, there is none more beautiful, none more inspiring than a lovely daughter of God who walks in virtue with an understanding of why she should do so, who honors and respects her body as a thing sacred and divine, who cultivates her mind and constantly enlarges the horizon of her understanding, who nurtures her spirit with everlasting truth."[39] Our bodies, our minds, and our spirits are what Father needs us to care for in order to be the mothers the children He has sent to our homes need.

As we have discussed, sacrifice is an essential eternal principle. It is beautiful! But just as we should embrace and incorporate our heaven-sent gifts, talents, and abilities, we should likewise embrace the minds, bodies, and spirits He has provided by caring for them.

Can we truly sacrifice in a state of emptiness? Satan twists our righteous desires to sacrifice for our families. The adversary enjoys sending the false message that sacrificing means we should neglect ourselves and that any sort of self-care is vain and selfish, leaving us deflated and full of guilt when we do take time for ourselves. If we are empty, Satan can find room for worldly

---

39 "Our Responsibility to Our Young Women," *Ensign*, September 1988.

outside sources to fill us. If we don't take time to sleep, he suggests we re-charge with unhealthy foods and drink. If we don't take time to play in enriching ways, we may end up zoning out on activities that don't matter much . . . just to get a little respite.

On multiple occasions within the scriptures, we are commanded to "love thy neighbour as thyself."[40] My worry is that if some of us followed that command, we wouldn't be very Christlike. In order to do as Christ wishes for our neighbor,

> On multiple occasions within the scriptures, we are commanded to "love thy neighbour as thyself." My worry is that if some of us followed that command, we wouldn't be very Christlike.

we *must* care for ourselves. As we strive to righteously sacrifice and seek out the one lost sheep, let us not forget that there are times when we ourselves are the ones who need attending to.

40 Matthew 22:39.

When we are cared for ourselves, we can care for our children in the way they deserve to be cared for. Remember, put the oxygen mask on yourself first! Two people not breathing isn't a very effective way to live.

Care for Our Bodies

We could all write an entire book on our relationships with our bodies, couldn't we? The books would be lengthy tomes. We'd talk about what our bodies looked like prior to breastfeeding three children. We'd lament that we have too much of this and not enough of that. If my academic research and research among friends is accurate, our books would likely include a lot of pain, a lot of negativity, and a lot of hopelessness in respect to our bodies.

I recently contacted over a hundred friends and asked their feelings regarding body image. The responses saddened, excited, depressed, and inspired me. I share their thoughts with mine within this section. Vulnerable topics are easier to talk about amongst friends. So if you are one of the 7–10 percent of women who love their bodies, stop right now, give thanks for this precious gift you have, and move on to the next section. For the remaining 90–93 percent of us, buckle up. It's about to get real.

Most of us can logically acknowledge that it doesn't matter what our bodies look like; it matters what they can do. We also know, however, that logic rarely transitions perfectly to emotion and belief.

On my social media post, my friend Tomi Ann Hill commented: "Believing the right things about your own body image is not always as easy as saying them to others."

The adversary wants us to hate our bodies. More than that, he wants us to *loathe* our bodies. He is seething with jealousy because he will never have one. He may rise to power with armies, money, and evil all around, but he will never feel his heart pump at the top of a breathtaking hike or know the joy of holding a human being he helped to create! If he can get the sorrow of fifteen extra pounds of baby fat to outweigh the joy of holding that baby, he wins. If he can make our hatred for our "big" nose more apparent in our minds than the smell of wet earth following a rainstorm, he wins. If he can make the guilt of eating taste so bitter that we don't taste the variety and deliciousness of our food, he wins.

"Do we really, truly understand how miraculous the body is? And if we don't, who is telling us so? I suggest it's someone who will never have a body and who is so jealous of the body that he will do all he can to make us hate ours," Sarah Wigington, another friend on social media, said. Friends, God is bigger. God is bigger than the adversary with the media and all of the other tools used against us in this war on our bodies. And we get to be the ones who decide who wins!

When we love something, we care for it. From the time we were little girls, we have heard that our bodies are temples.[41] This phrase isn't just a cultural phrase or vain repetition. The Bible Dictionary calls temples "the most holy of any place of worship."[42] We reside in holy houses of worship, and it is our job to love, care for, and treat them as such. Absolutely, we need to learn to love our bodies no matter their shape, size, or ability, but it is vital to also care for that body, no matter its shape, size, or ability.

Here are a few practical ideas for body self-care:

Prayer

I always start any epic life journey with prayer. Pour your soul out to Heavenly Father. Tell Him how you feel about your body and why. Ask Him for help as you begin to try to love and accept the body you have. *"Father, I am feeling so self-conscious*

---

41 See 1 Corinthians 6:19.

42 Bible Dictionary, "Temple."

about   this cesarean sec-tion   scar b e c a u s e my   stom-ach used to be flat and now there is this scar. It

> When we are internally and eternally motivated, progress seems to come naturally.

makes me feel like I am a different person. Can you help me, Father? Can you help me remember my trea-sured baby came from this scar? Can you help me love the hard things my body has done?"

Following your prayer, take a few minutes to sit in silence. Record the initial impressions you have.

Motivation

The key to success is your motivation and real-istic expectations—bodies are the Lord's hands to care for our (His) children. When our motivation is external, it is unhelpful, unsustainable, and un-realistic to progress and health. Conversely, when we are internally and eternally motivated, progress seems to come naturally. Elder Holland says, "In terms of preoccupation with self and a fixation on the physical, this is more than social insanity; it is spiritually destructive, and it accounts for much of the unhappiness women, including young women, face in the modern world. And if adults are preoccupied with appearance—tucking and nipping and implanting and remodeling everything that can be remodeled—those pressures and anxieties will certainly seep through to children."[43]

Examples of unhelpful motivation might include but are not limited to: attaining a certain societally prescribed size, weight, shape, or look; any comparison that incites a desire to look as good as or better than someone else; seeking approval; a desire to receive attention for outward appearance over internal beauty; anything external and prone to change.

Examples of helpful motivation might include but are not limited to: good health to be able to do the things we are called upon to do, an ability to do the things we love to do, a desire to remain with our families as long as possible on the earth, the drive to serve our families and communities, being good stewards of the bodies we were given, an intent to follow the Word of Wisdom, an intent to keep our minds clear to obtain learning, anything internally motivated and eternal.

---

43 "To Young Women," *Ensign*, November 2005.

Positive thinking and gratitude

Following my hysterectomy, I quickly gained twenty pounds. I was upset, sad, and worried, so I hired a personal trainer. During our third exercise session together, the trainer abruptly stopped and told me she could not sit there and listen to me talk about myself like "that" anymore. I hadn't even noticed what I was doing, but apparently, as I worked out, I was narrating all the horrible and disgusting things about my body. The trainer told me it was painful to listen to and it was actually hurting her spirit. From that moment on, she said I had to do burpees every time I was negative. In addition to the burpees, she more warmly challenged me to keep a body gratitude journal for thirty days. Each night before bed, I was to write three things I was grateful for about my body. Then came the ultimatum: either keep the journal or stop working out with her. I begrudgingly agreed to the journal.

It was a rocky start with the body gratitude journal. The first few days, I remember sitting there, pen in hand, writing the obvious: I'm thankful for my eyes. I'm thankful for my legs. I'm thankful for my arms. After about a week, all the obvious things were taken, and I was forced to think. "I'm thankful for the color of my eyes. I've always liked how brown they are!" Another week into the exercise, I began to see things during the day and was excited to write them down. "I am thankful for the spot right below my shoulder where my baby likes to bury his head as he falls asleep." By the end of the month, things I would normally put myself down about came to my mind as positives. The first time this happened, I was "running" on the treadmill (the quotes are included as I was going 4.25 miles per hour. Hey, it was running for me!) I felt my body bouncing up and down, and instead of my brain going automatically to its normal message of "Your fat is jiggling; how embarrassing for you!" it went to this thought, "Wow, my heart is beating so hard, and I love the rhythm of my bum bouncing on this treadmill. I am getting so strong." I felt thankful for my rear end! I kid you not!

In addition to body gratitude journaling, I also love a friend's idea to practice turning around my thoughts. Here's how: When a negative thought comes to your mind, stop and turn it around! "I look so fat" becomes "I just love how I look in these jeans." Even if you personally don't find it to be true (let's face it, you aren't a good judge of truth in these situations), just say the opposite thing. Your brain's neural pathways have been taught to feed

> As we practice mindful positivity regarding our thoughts, our practices and ultimately our beliefs, we will begin to see the great miracle our bodies are. From breathing to healing to pumping our hearts, we have been given bodies to house the souls that mother the children of God!

you negative thoughts and must be rewired to instinctively go to positive thoughts. This process of neural rewiring takes about thirty days. Soon you will notice positive thoughts coming to mind as easily as your negative thoughts came in the past.

Our brains are powerful. We have the God-given gift of creation, and that includes the creation of our thoughts. Mahatma Gandhi said, "Your beliefs become your thoughts. Your thoughts become your words. Your words become your actions. Your actions become your habits. Your habits become your values. Your values become your destiny."[44] As we practice mindful positivity regarding our thoughts,

44 http://www.quotationspage.com/quote/36464.html. This quote is often misattributed to Margaret Thatcher.

our practices and ultimately our beliefs, we will begin to see the great miracle our bodies are. From breathing to healing to pumping our hearts, we have been given bodies to house the souls that mother the children of God!

Throw away your scale

I'm just going to say it: weight is not an

> Weight is not an accurate measurement of your worth. It never has been and never will be. Thinking that you will be happy when you finally lose the weight is a lie and does not come from the source of truth and light.

accurate measurement of your worth. It never has been and never will be. Thinking that you will be happy when you finally lose the weight is a lie and does not come from the source of truth and light.

There have been two times in my adult life when I have reached my "perfect" weight. (Which, incidentally, in my societally conditioned mind was my high-school weight at age fifteen.) The first time was when I was so sick with a pregnancy that I was malnourished and required nutrition through medical intervention. The second was several years ago when I was tired of what I, in a derogatory manner, called "the mom-bod" and determined that through hard work I could be a certain number of pounds again. After all, the charts I looked up online all said my weight goal was within the healthy range for my height, so in my mind, it was a reasonable aspiration. Never mind the fact that the Internet really knows nothing about me, my shape, my heredity, etc.

Reaching this ridiculous weight required ninety-plus minutes in the gym daily, a personal trainer, as well as a gym pass, carefully tracking every drop of water and every milligram of food that went into my body, missing out on dinner parties and social events, about three hours of meal preparation per day, and an obsessive weekly date with my scale.

If the number on the scale went down that week, I told myself all the work I had done was sufficient. I would be really "good" the next week in my eating and exercise. If the number on the scale went up, I told myself nothing I had done was good enough. I would comfort myself with poor food choices and convince myself I didn't feel like exercising. I based my self-worth on the scale! Remember we learned in chapter two that worth cannot go up and down?

Imagine my surprise and sadness when I finally reached the high school weight. Yes, I looked what the world called better. But inside I was the same. It was a very dark time in my life.

Some years later, I had an experience where I found peace with my body. We had just moved from one house to another, and the scale was packed in a box that had gotten misplaced in the move. It was an expensive scale, and I knew I would find it eventually, so I didn't bother replacing it and just went about my life. I fed my body when it was hungry. I remained active throughout the day, unpacking and completing my tasks in my role as a mom. I was doing fitness classes I enjoyed. For the first time in years, I was in a mental sweet spot regarding my physical appearance. I recognized that my clothes were a little looser but didn't think much of it. Then one day, many weeks later, I found the scale, jumped on it, and saw that I was but a few pounds more than what I considered my optimal weight. I was shocked. How had this happened? I hadn't starved myself on the diet of the month. I had eaten *normally* with my family . . . and sometimes I had even had *salad dressing, for heaven's sake!* It became clear to me that peace with my body was healthy. When I was at peace with my mind and body, I made good choices—I stopped when I was full, was active, engaged in exercise I actually enjoyed, and didn't put myself down all the time.

> Throw away the scale! We don't need scales. We can get our weight once a year in the doctor's office and can easily estimate our weight if needed in other circumstances. Let's stop giving power to a small household appliance and instead worry more about loving the skin we are in.

A happy story, right? But then, of course, I had found the scale again, so the vicious cycle returned.

Every doctor will tell us the following: muscle weighs more than fat but takes up less space. Body mass index is not an accurate determination of health. Body fat percentage is a much more accurate determination. And yet we still give power to a scale!

Throw away the scale! We don't need scales. We can get our weight once a year in the doctor's office and can easily estimate our weight if needed in other circumstances. Let's stop giving power to a small household appliance and instead worry more about loving the skin we are in.

Eat, drink, exercise, sleep

As mothers, let us choose to nourish ourselves instead of feeding our emotions. And for once, can we please enjoy eating without the guilt? Our loving Father and His Son's plan for us is to have bodies that have to be fed every few hours to sustain themselves. Is it our belief that they wanted us to feel guilty three to six times daily for seventy-plus years? Guilt over our eating leads to unhealthy behavior and self-deprecation and furthers our unhealthy eating

> When we eat to mindfully and joyfully nourish our bodies, we are naturally healthier in our choices.

habits. When we eat to mindfully and joyfully nourish our bodies, we are naturally healthier in our choices.

As mothers, may we pour enough water into our bodies to keep them hydrated and functioning. Yes, there was a time in my life when I believed my body was made up of 60 percent "Dirty Dr. Pepper" (a coconut-flavored soda). Not so, apparently. As it turns out, my body is actually made up of 60 percent water and feels much better when I hydrate it.

As mothers, let's pump our hearts and build our muscles doing things we love! If you hate running, *stop running*. Go to yoga, dance, hike, or ride a bike instead. When we torture ourselves with exercise we hate, we tell our bodies we don't care what they think. Exercise by doing whatever it is that opens your heart to make you feel wholly connected with your body, mind, and spirit while you are doing it.

One of the most poignant insights on my social media post came from my friend Lanee Miller, who said, "It wasn't until I did things that helped me appreciate my body that I really started loving it more, like when I skied, something I was afraid of; or when I finally did a yoga pose I didn't think I could do; or had babies; or when I focused more on the amazing opportunities my body allowed me instead of always seeing only what I looked like. I'm grateful for a body that works and will let me challenge it. I try to remember those moments so I have a defense when I look in the mirror and want to lose 'vanity pounds.'"

There is beautiful symbolism in eating, drinking, exercising, and sleeping. Our need to continually drink water is mirrored in our need to constantly return to the Living Water—the Savior and His teachings. Our need to eat constantly reminds us that we are to "feast upon the words of Christ."[45] Our need to pump our heart and build our muscles is a metaphor for weak things becoming strong.[46] These are but a few of the many symbols relating to our bodies.

Instead of obsessively measuring each calorie, each ounce of water, each minute exercised, or each moment slept, we would be wise to focus on health and eternal goals. When it comes to goal setting, less is more. If you conquer something quickly, great! You can set new goals. But setting yourself up with seven thousand tasks to be checked off each day will only lead to failure or exhaustion. There is power in focusing on one thing at a time. If you

45 2 Nephi 32:3.

46 See Ether 12:27.

choose to focus on drinking more water, watch what happens around you! A great article might come up on your social media news feed about water, you'll hear a song that reminds you of the symbolic nature of water. Led by the Spirit, your whole world will come together to help you attain your goal. Spreading our focus too thin can make it hard to hear, see, and feel the messages around us from the Spirit.

> Led by the Spirit, your whole world will come together to help you attain your goal. Spreading our focus too thin can make it hard to hear, see, and feel the messages around us from the Spirit. So set small, focused goals, and remember to let God know your plan. He's the best accountability partner and workout buddy there is!

So set small, focused goals, and remember to let God know your plan. He's the best accountability partner and workout buddy there is!

Eternally motivated goals for health may include: I'm going to stop measuring every calorie and become mindful of my eating, and I'm going to stop when I'm full. Rather than measure each ounce of water I take in, I'm going to drink a large glass of water when I wake up in the morning and then every time I eat, and I'm going to carry a water bottle with me. Instead of that awful 5:00 a.m. boot-camp class I hate, I am going to go to yoga. I love it there. I'm going to get as much sleep as I (a mother) can tonight, and if I need a power nap or early bedtime tomorrow, I'm not going to make myself feel guilty over it.

Yes, it is important to try

No, we do not buy into the world's view that looks are what matter. We truly believe, as writer Stephanie Nielsen has said, that "it's a beautiful heart, not a perfect body, that leads to a beautiful life."[47] However, we do believe in taking care of our bodies the best that we can. When it comes to our physical presentation, it actually is important to try.

If we all agree that our bodies are temples, let's look to how we care for our temples as our guide.

---

47 *Heaven Is Here: An Incredible Story of Hope, Triumph, and Everyday Joy* (New York City: Hachette Books, 2012).

A temple is built with products that are of the best quality within a reasonable budget. It is modestly decorated but with care. And every year, often twice a year, the temple undergoes a resting period, where it is deep-cleaned and restored. I like to tell my family that the temple shuts down for a few days every year for maintenance, and so do I!

When I first became a stay-at-home (and work-from-home) mother, I found the all-day-sweats, grease-head, no-makeup look to be refreshing. After a few months, though, it got old. I found myself less productive and less social. What was the point of getting ready anyway? No one's around to see me. When someone knocked on my door, I didn't always answer it. I had a *tiny* semblance of self-respect and didn't want the neighbor to see me like this at four in the afternoon, for Pete's sake! Walking outside required pants, so I *obviously* wasn't going to do that. I did a lot of puttering about the house those days.

I like to tell my family that the temple shuts down for a few days every year for maintenance, and so do I!

I finally recognized this as a problem and, true to my m.o., started reading about it. One author suggested that whatever I did in the morning, I needed to put on my athletic shoes. It seemed simple to me, but it worked! I was more productive. Soon I was getting dressed again, and I was so much happier. No one's around to see you anyway? Wrong. *You* are around to see you. So are your kiddos.

Don't get me wrong. I love a jammie day every once in awhile. I still take a couple of those a month. In fact, I'm writing now in fuzzy socks with a 1990s scrunchie on my head. But my jammie days are now part of my self-care when I need a little TLC and not the norm.

Everyone's "temple maintenance" program will look a little different, and that is okay. We have enough to do. Let's not waste time worrying about who is doing what or why or if that's really what God wants.

Two of my friends recently had a heated debate on social media about an eyelash trend. One was pro. One was against. And they went at it. Eventually they started questioning each other's motives. I deleted the post and wrote each of them a personal note expressing my love for them. It left me sad. I know and love both of these women, but they didn't know each other. The great irony is that in knowing both of them, I know they would really like each other.

Whose beautiful soul are we missing in our judgments? It is possible to put on nice clothes and makeup without being self-absorbed, and it is possible to do those things with inappropriate self-focus. Someone can wear no makeup at all and care for their body while someone doing the same thing is actually neglecting themself. We don't really know what's happening in people's minds, do we? The answer to what motivates a person is found in their heart. As none of us is in possession of heart-vision goggles, let's just think the best of the women around us as we try to love each other better.

> The answer to what motivates a person is found in their heart. As none of us is in possession of heart-vision goggles, let's just think the best of the women around us as we try to love each other better.

When you are getting ready in the morning, what are you thinking about yourself?

My daughter is a science nut. Truly a nut. We once had twelve tomato plants growing in our office from November until the week after Mother's Day. My entire house smelled "of the earth." And it was all so my little brainiac could prove what temperature of water was best for growing plants. It was her first science-fair project.

When we went to the science fair at the school to view all of the kids' projects, I saw one that caught my eye. One child had done an experiment to prove that speaking positively to droplets of water made more beautiful ice. The student had spoken positive words to one tray of water droplets and negative words to the other. The droplets were then frozen under the same conditions and subsequently viewed under a microscope. Results from the droplets were significantly different. The positive droplets were beautiful, with intricate crystals, whereas the negative droplets looked like blobs of ice.

I was fascinated. I came home and, thanks to Google, found the origin of the experiment. Dr. Masaru Emoto is a Japanese scientist who has devoted study to the power of positive thinking. When you go to the science fair with your kids and see the "rice project" or the "water droplet project," you have Dr. Emoto to thank! He proved that positivity in word and thought has the power to change the very composition of matter.

Though getting-ready routines can widely differ, most of us stand in front of the mirror at some point in the process. What if we spent those minutes while we got ready speaking positively to ourselves? Look into the mirror and tell yourself what beautiful things God made when He created your body, mind, and spirit.

My self-maintenance rituals include nightly baths, a specific kind of lipstick I love, and putting together great outfits by copying things I see on Pinterest.

My sister-in-law's self-maintenance program includes gorgeous eyelashes she does herself, knowing and sporting the latest styles, and doing TV yoga after the kids are in bed.

Another sister-in-law loves makeup and always knows the latest makeup trends and styles. My birthday presents from her are always one of her favorite new gadgets: hair tools, makeup, fun jewelry.

A friend of mine gets a pedicure once a month. Another friend is passionate about her eyebrows. One of my friends does no makeup at all but buys great moisturizer and lip balm.

And I say bravo to all! Love and care for that skin (that temple) you're in!

Recognize that loving your body is a process

Our children are watching us. We have within us the power to shape the way our sons see the women in their lives and the relationships our daughters have with their own bodies. (It should be noted that problems with body image are not for our daughters alone. Body image is an issue that crosses gender lines. Our sons are watching as well.) Out of the scores of women I have spoken with on this topic, many told me their own experiences of body image—both positive and negative—can be traced to the way their mothers related to their own bodies.

On my social media inquiry, Julie Webb noted, "I went through a chubby phase in high school. All of my sisters did too, but we never even knew it! People at school would talk about gaining weight, but it never occurred to me that I should worry about it. This is thanks to my mother. Bodies were things we never talked badly of in our home. Mom told all of us we were great, and she thought she was great too! I've taken this attitude into parenting my own five daughters."

In his bold, powerful, and never-mincing-words way, Elder Holland said this on the subject:

I plead with you young women to please be more accepting of yourselves, including your body shape and style, with a little less longing to look like someone else. We are all different. Some are tall, and some are short. Some are round, and some are thin. And almost everyone at some time or other wants to be something they are not! . . . Every young woman is a child of destiny and every adult woman a powerful force for good. I mention adult women because, sisters, you are our greatest examples and resource for these young women. And if you are obsessing over being a size 2, you won't be very surprised when your daughter or the Mia Maid in your class does the same and makes herself physically ill trying to accomplish it. We should all be as fit as we can be—that's good Word of Wisdom doctrine. That means eating right

and exercising and helping our
bodies function at their optimum
strength. We could probably all do
better in that regard. But I speak
here of optimum health; there is
no universal optimum size.[48]

If you are struggling with body image or practicing care of your physical body, you aren't alone.
And you are still the mother your children need.
Let them see you choose to stop thinking poorly
of yourself. Let them see you choose to care for
your body. Let them see you on this journey of
self-love and acceptance. Watching you use the
Atonement of Jesus Christ in coming to love and
accept your body will be just as powerful and lasting a message to them as what they would receive
from someone to whom body love and care come
naturally.

Who are we to say what a perfected body looks
like? What if all the things we can't wait to get rid
of—the cellulite, the scars, the imperfect this or
that—actually are perfect? Perhaps your body gave
life and is now scarred and stretched. Maybe your
body was built to be a strong and solid daughter of
God when the world tells you to be small. Maybe

---

48 "To Young Women," *Ensign*, November 2005.

you struggle with emotional and chemical mental health challenges that leave you drained but also allow you to feel deeply for your children in a way God needs you to be able to feel. Jesus, our Savior, was resurrected, and with power to do anything, He kept His scars on His perfected body. Would we? Our Savior wanted us to remember what He did for us, so He wears us forever on His hands. I wear the scars of my motherhood on my body. And that, my sisters, is beautiful.

Care for our minds

I always planned on being a highly educated person. A bachelor's degree was a must; graduate

Jesus, our Savior, was resurrected, and with power to do anything, He kept His scars on His perfected body. Would we? Our Savior wanted us to remember what He did for us, so He wears us forever on His hands. I wear the scars of my motherhood on my body. And that, my sisters, is beautiful.

work was optional. That was not where I found myself in my early twenties. Instead, I found myself out of college, without a degree, and unable to return to school at that time to obtain one. As a former high school honor student and lover of learning, I was despondent.

I sat on my porch on a warm summer evening just as the stars were appearing. I was feeling quite sorry for myself when I read these words by Sister Marjorie Pay Hinckley:

> I had hoped to go to the University of Utah. But the year was 1929 "the bottom of the depression." On the day I registered for classes I returned home to find that the company my father had been working for as an accountant had gone bankrupt and closed. He was out of work. The next day I withdrew from the university, went downtown, and miraculously secured a job as a secretary. Since college was not an option, I decided, well, if this is my life, I'd better educate myself. And I worked hard at it. I read and I read and I read.[49]

---

49 *Glimpses* (Salt Lake City: Deseret Book Company 1999), 96–97.

If Sister Hinckley could be well-educated in spite of her situation, I could be educated too. I read everything I could get my hands on. I took community education classes at local universities. My new husband was busy at school obtaining his bachelor of science degree in psychology at the time, and seeing the many hours of studying required of him, I turned it into an opportunity for my own intellectual growth. I began to study with him. I read his textbooks. I completed his assignments parallel to his completion of them. We had long talks about what he was learning. Although my assignments were never turned in and I was never graded, I feel that my vicarious education from that time has served me well.

Knowledge is one of the few things we get to take with us from this life. Part of our self-care is giving ourselves permission to stretch our minds and obtain as much knowledge as we can.

Being a mom, I sometimes feel like the only intellectual stimulation I get is from my children's favorite television shows, although I can't deny I have learned a thing or two from *Super Why*. Our minds are capable of so much more than we give them! There are always new ways to learn, even in short bursts. Technology is an amazing tool! I love listening to podcasts, taking classes in my community, listening to audiobooks as I clean the house, and reading my favorite poetry to my kids. Our brains are not dead. Even if one more episode of your kid's show of the week makes you think it is!

The more we learn about the gospel and the world around us, the more capable we become. With our capability, we are able to love and serve better. Most importantly, however, we are much more capable mothers. Learn all you can right now, however that looks in your current situation. If Sister Hinckley could do it in the midst of a great depression, we can too!

Care for our spirits

We go to church weekly. When we come home with our kids in tow, there really should be fans cheering us on as we pull into our driveway. Throngs of people clapping for a job well done. . . . We survived. From the time your baby is mobile until they go to nursery, you can pretty much forget about any sort of normal Church experience. Then there are a few blissful years of relatively good behavior before you have to start monitoring sacrament meeting electronic usage. Pile that on top of getting the kids ready for church, an early-morning meeting, choir practice, the lesson you have to teach the third hour, subbing in Primary the second hour, and helping your middle child give the prayer in their Primary class. It is busy and noisy. Yet this is the only time in the week that many of us have set aside for the care of our spirits! Even when we do get a solid three-hour block of spiritual feasting, it isn't enough to last a week.

We know what it feels like when our spirits are tired and so, so thirsty. If someone told us we could drink only once a week, we would think they were ridiculous. Everyone knows we need daily water to survive and eight glasses a day for good health. How could we possibly think that drinking once a week at church on Sunday from the fountain of living waters is enough? The living waters "are a representation of the love of God." [50] We need the love of God many times a day to hydrate our spirits to give them strength to face the world in front of us.

I know a few things about spiritual dehydration. There were a few years in my life when my questions left me thirsting. I asked Christ to walk with me, but I couldn't find Him anywhere. I wondered if I ever would. Notwithstanding this dark fear, I knew He and Heavenly Father loved me. I knew I was a child of God. It was just that They felt so . . . out of reach. Didn't They know I was being bombarded and I needed Them? I wanted answers. I wanted Christ's companionship. I didn't just want the *idea* of Christ. I wanted a personal, one-on-one relationship with Him!

50 See 1 Nephi 11:25.

Faithfully, I sought Him, even when things were foggy and confusing with what I perceived as little hope of success. With consistent devotion to my spiritual-care practices and in spite of deeply seated fear and doubt, I finally found Him again. I would say He found me, but the truth of the matter is that He had always known where I was. For, as Elder Holland testifies, "No one can fall lower than the light of Christ shines. That isn't possible."[51] He was with me all along.

> I sought Him, even when things were foggy and confusing with what I perceived as little hope of success. With consistent devotion to my spiritual-care practices and in spite of deeply seated fear and doubt, I finally found Him again.

I found Him again in a yoga class, of all places! There I was in an awkward downward dog pose, and from nowhere, His love filled me with one of the most sacred spiritual experiences of my life. With excitement and relief, I started to see Him

51 "The Savior Understands Me," https://www.lds.org/media-library/video/2016-03-0021.

everywhere. The wall around my heart crumbled. Each time I found Him, another brick fell. He was in the temple and the mountains, in nature, in music, and not in a metaphorical way! "Salvation is a personal, individual experience. . . . This is a very personal relationship with Christ. The Savior understands us because He is not an abstraction."[52]

My searching for Him had been continuous, and I kept coming up empty-handed, or so I thought. Through consistent work on my part, the Savior and I had finally developed enough of a relationship for me to recognize His presence! Christ gave His life for the plan of agency, for *our* agency, so we can't really blame Him if He'd like an invitation to walk with us. Habitual spiritual development is the invitation He is looking for.

A consistent routine of reaching out to Christ with spiritual self-care practices helps us recognize who we are seeing when we see Him, who we are hearing when we hear Him, who we are feeling when we feel Him. It's always Christ. He's never actually left your side. He is with you everywhere.

Each of us gets to develop her own spiritual self-care routine. My spiritual self-care practice looks like this:

I know it's a challenge with kids, but I try my very hardest to make the fifteen minutes of the

---

52 Ibid.

sacrament ordinance matter. Even if my children are being difficult, I focus on going inward. If the only spiritual connection I get during church is those fifteen sacrament minutes, I call it a success.

In the morning, I spend about ten minutes alone before or after my kids have gone to school. I pray, read a few scriptures, do a yoga sequence, and drink a big glass of water.

Throughout the day, I try to turn my focus to Him as much as possible. The things I do often include a few of the following: I work to keep a prayer in my heart by constantly dialoguing with Heavenly Father. I pray when I eat. When I see something beautiful, I try to give thanks for it. I sing in the shower. While doing laundry and housework, I listen to talks on lds.org or programs on The Mormon Channel. Whenever possible, I attend the temple. On my bathroom mirror is a picture of the Savior. I seek opportunities to be outside my house, in nature, without electronics because God, the Savior, and the Holy Ghost are found in quiet places.

Before bed, I spend conscientious time winding down. Sometimes I read another scripture, talk, or thought. I may listen to music. I meditate. I honestly speak aloud with my Heavenly Father—free from posturing. I tell Him like it is and then listen. If I have any impressions, I write them down. My husband and I have our prayer together, and then we go to bed.

I do these things when I want to, but more importantly, I do them when I *don't* want to do them. That's when I actually need them most. Seeking a connection to heaven unites my spirit, mind, and body in a way that makes me feel whole—authentic.

When I feel whole, there is nothing I cannot do. Authenticity is the best missionary tool we have because it draws people to us as they see us as we really are: connected in mind, body, and spirit and full of testimony.

When our children wonder what makes us so happy, we can tell them honestly that we make our personal relationships with Heavenly Father and Jesus Christ a priority in our lives. We call for them many times a day, and they answer our calls, filling us with light, knowledge, answers, and strength.

Elder Holland reminds us:

> Christ does know us. He has walked the thorny, difficult, rock-strewn path of our lives. How he did that I don't know . . . God loved me in a sense, almost as much as He loved his only begotten son. At least I can say this:

> When our children wonder what makes us so happy, we can tell them honestly that we make our personal relationships with Heavenly Father and Jesus Christ a priority in our lives. We call for them many times a day, and they answer our calls, filling us with light, knowledge, answers, and strength.

He gave His only begotten son, for me. And that says something about my worth in His eyes and my worth in the eyes of the Savior. . . . What it means to me is that He understands me, that He loves me and that He reaches me. So I can't explain how that happens, I just know that it does.[53]

* * *

This past year, my husband and I decided that as part of my self-care, I would go on a retreat. We

53 Ibid.

have stopped giving each other material gifts on holidays and instead give each other experiences. I saved up a birthday, a Mother's Day, and two anniversaries for this!

On the retreat, I slept for eight luxurious hours for three nights and took naps in the afternoon. I ate organic food that someone else prepared for me and hiked more than twelve miles through golden quaking aspens. I spent time praying, pondering, reading scripture, meditating, reading a book, listening to poetry, and conversing with wise women. I did a two-hour yoga practice each morning and evening and connected with my body. I went to the retreat with a specific problem in mind that I wanted heavenly help with. I treated myself to a massage and bought myself a new outfit. I wrote in the evenings, spent a lot of time alone, and even jumped from a rope swing into a lake. Alone in my room at nights, I laughed deeply and cried until there weren't tears left to cry. There was so much quiet that I got answers to the specific problem I brought with me and to other looming questions I had. I connected to the essential part of myself that sometimes gets lost in the ceaseless busyness of life. I came home from the retreat with my bucket full to overflowing, ready to wife and mother another day! It was about $400 for four days, and it was worth every cent.

This is an extravagant example for me, probably for most of us, and it is unsustainable in a day-to-day, real-life setting, but it was perhaps more valuable because it lasted but a moment. Most of the time, my self-care routine involves taking a bath without anyone banging on the wall and asking me to sign the permission slip they just slid under the bathroom door. When I was a nursing mom, any self-care had to be done in rare, in-between-feeding, ninety-minute bursts. There is a time and a season for everything. God was on my retreat with me, but He is also in my closet when I have a moment to pray alone. He is with me when I listen to an inspirational talk while the baby naps. He whispers answers to prayer in the wind while I walk around the block. He is where quiet is and where the world is not.

As with anything we give our precious time to, it is important to approach self-care with thoughtful consideration. Decisions on how much time we devote, what specifically we do, and how much is too much within our self-care practice are personal. They are between us, God, and our spouse, if married. Heavenly Father is aware of our individual circumstances and is waiting to help us! Through the Holy Ghost, we can come to know what is just right for our own families and situations.

> We cannot care for the needs of others if we are an empty and hollow shell. I want to be physically, mentally, and spiritually healthy so I am capable of placing my will on God's altar.

Our motivation for self-care is not to gain approval from the world. Our motivation is the desire to be healthy enough to fulfill our divine missions and teach our children likewise. We cannot care for the needs of others if we are an empty and hollow shell. I want to be physically, mentally, and spiritually healthy so I am capable of placing my will on God's altar.

At the end of my life, I want to be able to say, "Father, I lovingly cared for this beautiful body, mind, and spirit you gave me. I cared for my body by feeding it well—often and with the best foods—by drinking water, by pumping my heart, by stretching my muscles, by learning to truly love what the world calls 'flaws,' like my stretch marks and cellulite, I worked hard, I played hard. I cared for my mind by learning all I could about the things I was drawn to, by asking for help when I needed it, by educating it with the best books, by asking questions, by seeking truth, by not shrinking, by maintaining a positive mind-set. I cared for my spirit by finding you and your Son everywhere I could. I found you in prayer, in meditation, in scripture, in the temple, in church, in nature, in quiet time alone, in my children, and in others I love. When I found you, I was made whole. And while I was caring for myself, I still chose you, Father! I was physically able, so I used this body to serve your children. I was mentally cared for, so I used my mind to learn of you and then teach others what I knew. I made spiritual development essential, so I testified of our relationship to all who knew me, and because I testified, they also came to know you. All that I did, Father, was meant to bring people—especially the little people you entrusted to me—back to you." If I can say that someday, my self-care will not have been wasted.

When I found you, I was made whole.

Chapter 7
Does God Want Me to Be Perfect?
Practicing Failure

"The real questions for parents should be: 'Are you engaged? Are you paying attention?' If so, plan to make lots of mistakes and bad decisions. Imperfect parenting moments turn into gifts as our children watch us try to figure out what went wrong and how we can do better next time. The mandate is not to be perfect and raise happy children. Perfection doesn't exist, and I've found what makes children happy doesn't always prepare them to be courageous, engaged adults."[54]

—Brené Brown

I was once a perfect mother. You were one too, remember? It was before you actually became one.

---

54 *Daring Greatly: How the Courage to Be Vulnerable Transforms the Way We Live, Love, Parent, and Lead* (New York City: Avery Books, 2015).

You had so many judgments, so many things to say. It usually went something like this. "When I am a mother, I am never going to_____" or "When I am a mother, I will always_____." It all looked so easy from where we stood, there on the outside. And so we wrote scripts for happy little stories of perfect parenting. It took us about one day of being mothers to realize how delusional we had been.

For me, that moment came when it was time to leave the hospital after having given birth to my first baby. It was discharge day, and the baby was all dressed in her "going home" outfit, with coordinating hair bow and blanket. The hospital personnel asked my husband and me to watch a film produced circa 1984 about the dangers of shaking our baby. We then signed a paper saying we would not shake our baby. And then the words, "You can go home now" came. Wait a sec! Wasn't someone going to give me a pep talk, give me a speech, give me a manual? No, they gave me a *human being*. According to them, I was a mom.

We can all have a good laugh now at our own naiveté, but the sad thing is that many of us have taken those judgments from our pre-mommy days and heaped them onto ourselves in our present-day mothering. We have to learn to say good-bye to what we thought motherhood was so we can love what motherhood is. It's no easy task! From birth, we watched our mothers and the other mothers around us. We were immersed in

> We have to learn to say good-bye to what we thought motherhood was so we can love what motherhood is.

our culture of perfectionism. We spent our entire lives pre-motherhood subconsciously scripting for ourselves what motherhood was supposed to be. At times, our scripts show us that we, or perhaps even our children, don't meet our own unrealistic expectations, so we feel ashamed.

Let's be clear about something right here, right now: shame is not of God. Shame is dark and ugly. Shame is a tool of Satan introduced to humankind in the Garden of Eden by a jealous and cunning adversary. We read in Genesis 2:25 that before Satan introduced shame, "they were both naked, the man and his wife, and were not ashamed." And then, after Adam and Eve were beguiled, we read in Genesis 3:10–13: "And he said, I heard thy voice in the garden, and I was afraid, because I was naked; and

I hid myself. And he said, Who told thee that thou wast naked? Hast thou eaten of the tree, whereof I commanded thee that thou shouldest not eat? And the man said, The woman whom thou gavest to be with me, she gave me of the tree, and I did eat. And the Lord God said unto the woman, What is this that thou hast done? And the woman said, The serpent beguiled me, and I did eat."

You see? It was Satan! He is the one who tells us we are naked and to hide when we fall short. Mistakes buried and covered up in shame breed perfectionism.

Godly sorrow, on the other hand, is from our Father in Heaven and is given to us in love. Godly sorrow inspires us to change. It encourages us to bring our failings into the light, where we can learn from them; where, through the Atonement of Jesus Christ, we can repent of them; and where we can ultimately heal from them. Making mistakes that cause us godly sorrow, which then inspires us to use the Atonement, are priceless experiences. Mistakes can increase our testimonies, helping us become more like Christ and the person He means us to be.

This is sure: shame equals hiding, and godly sorrow equals healing.

Yet, so many times we choose to hide in shame instead of heal in light. Why? In the honest places of our hearts, we know why. We hide because no matter who we are or what we have done, we were born with the light of Christ. This light, even if buried deep inside, causes us to know and, therefore, love Him. In knowing Him, we don't want to disappoint Him. We hide because it is vulnerable to say we did wrong and we are in need of His help. It is at times easier to hide in the pit of shame than to face the pain that comes from knowing our

It is at times easier to hide in the pit of shame than to face the pain that comes from knowing our own actions caused part of His suffering. We hide because we are afraid that if He sees our imperfection, He can't possibly love us, and, oh, how we need His love. The simple truth is that He already knows. He has seen our failings, even the ones we are trying to hide. And the miracle of it all is that He still loves us.

own actions caused part of His suffering. We hide because we are afraid that if He sees our imperfection, He can't possibly love us, and, *oh, how we need His love*. The simple truth is that He already knows. He has seen our failings, even the ones we are trying to hide. And the miracle of it all is that He still loves us.

Shame tells us we are not enough. It wants us to forget the divine nature we are working to embrace. We have to put shame and perfectionism out of our lives for good. Mothering in perfectionism is a miserable business. We *know* we will never attain perfection in this life. There was but one perfect Being to walk the earth, and He was perfect so that we don't have to be!

What would it be like if we allowed our children to watch us sin, feel godly sorrow, and use the Atonement to repent and heal? Allowing our children to see us when we make a mistake humanizes us. Instead of a foe, we become to our children a mother who is a safe haven when they have themselves gone wrong. Feigning our own perfection will not prevent our children from missteps. It will just prevent them from telling us about them. When we don't know, we can't help. When we do know, we can teach. How better to lead than by loving example?

* * *

The Atonement covers all failure. Not only can the Atonement heal us from sin failures because of our choices, but it also covers the vulnerability that comes from taking chances and failing!

I love the story of Jia Jang, an entrepreneur from China. He had a big American dream, and when he got here, he found that his dream wasn't so easily attained. He kept failing and was on the verge of giving up and settling, but his wife encouraged him to take six months to try to get his dream business going again. After four of the six months had passed, he came upon something known as rejection therapy.

In essence, rejection therapy encourages people to practice failure so it doesn't hurt as much. Jia decided to practice this rejection therapy for ninety days by setting out to be rejected everywhere he went. He asked people for ridiculous things. He attempted crazy feats. He spent ninety days asking for things so outlandish he would most certainly be rejected.

What he encountered was fascinating. Although he was rejected and failed many times, he actually succeeded many more times than he thought he would. He said, "I was blown away at how kind society is to me. I didn't know that before."

I first heard Jia Jang's story in 2014. I was going through a period of self-reflection concerning the way we lived as a family. I decided to revolutionize the way I mothered. Jia Jang and others I studied were experiencing lives of meaning and purpose because they had made failure a safe part of their human experience, and I wondered what it would look like in our family to make failure safe and to learn to let the Atonement make us brave.

I knew the world out there wanted to tear my babies down and fill them with shame. But I would have none of that! My children loved getting medals and awards, so I decided we needed an award to celebrate our failures.

We went to Deseret Industries thrift store to find an old trophy we fully intended to spray paint later. After twelve point seven long seconds of searching, we found it. It was an old piano trophy upon which were etched the words "Piano Festival 2008, 100 Point Solo JOSH BARLOW." It found a home with us. We call it The Josh Barlow Trophy of Failure or The Josh Barlow Trophy, for short. Our original plan to spray paint it drifted away to the hole of good intentions. The name had already stuck.

The Josh Barlow Trophy helps us celebrate our family's epic failures. Whenever someone at our house makes a mistake, or as my daughter says, "fails big-time," we celebrate, and the individual who failed gets to carry the trophy around with them for a day or so. People put notes and treats in it. It sits at their place at the dinner table. We talk about it, laugh about it, and cheer on the failure. We learn together that failing is a really cool and important part of life.

Take that, world.

When my kids leave this house, I don't want them to feel like failure is wrong. I need them to understand that they will experience failure on the road to success. I myself often have failures. One night I gathered the kids together and held the trophy as I told them that in life, some days are Josh Barlow Trophy days, so I was celebrating. I told them how passionately I felt about the things I'd failed at and how proud I was of the work I had put into the failures. I let them see how sad I was about failing. I allowed them to see my hurt to remind them that being brave and vulnerable hurts sometimes.

Then I told them how excited I was to find out what would come next. I reminded them it was going to feel so sweet the next time something good came around . . . and I knew that it would. I pointed out that it was a gift to be able to see that my failure and sadness meant the success and happiness of another and that I could still be happy for that other person. We got to talk about what God has planned for me instead and the faith it requires to go forward in that direction. I don't know if they listened, but I told them. Or maybe I told myself.

Take time to go to your local thrift store. Pick up a trophy. Reward your kids for taking on the big, bad world. Sometimes when you fail, something as simple as a cheap plastic trophy that formerly belonged to a pianist named Josh Barlow makes it easier to get back on your feet again.

I'm not the only mom celebrating failure. Sara Blakely is a mother of four and owner of Spanx shapewear. She was listed by both *Times* and *Forbes* magazines as one of the most powerful and influential women in the world. When she was asked how she was able to attain her level of success, she referenced her father.

This remarkable father would sit at the dinner table with his children and ask them to talk about their failures. "He'd actually be disappointed if I didn't have something I'd failed at that week," Sara said. After years of professional failures, Sara has become one of the only female self-made billionaires in the world. At business meetings and in her own home, she celebrates with her employees and her children what she calls the "oops" moments. Just like her dad.

(Incidentally, I despise Sara's product. The first time I wore Spanx, I actually went into the back room and ripped them off of my body in front of all the white-gloved caterers at a Gala for the opening of a fancy art gallery. Yes, right off my body, there in the middle of the éclair decorating station. The second time I wore them was to my very romantic fifteenth wedding anniversary dinner at a swanky city restaurant. The restaurant was serving a seven-course meal that night. At course two, things got uncomfortable. At course three, things hurt. At course four, the food simply had nowhere else to go. In great pain, I made a quick dash for the bathroom, peeled the Spanx off with a sigh of relief, and—having nowhere to put them—shoved them in the sleeve of my dress. With one arm looking normal and the other looking three times its size, I returned to the table. My advice to my husband as he stared in horror and confusion at my arm was, "Don't. Even. Ask." I spent the remaining three courses of the meal with shapewear threatening to peek out of my sleeve. No more shoving our bodies into those things, say I! Long live body ripples! But that is neither here nor there. Good on Sara for celebrating failure, and she can laugh at my stories all the way to the bank.)

In being willing to try, fail, hurt . . . then get back up, we teach our children it is safe for them to do the same. It is okay when they don't win the reflections contest at school, when they don't get picked for the team, when the boy they asked to the Sadie Hawkins dance says no. When we make failure a safe practice in our homes, we teach that worth isn't something we have to hustle for. In failure or success, worth is worth and does not change.

None of these stories should be interpreted as a suggestion that we should promote laziness, apathy, or premeditated sin as acceptable traits in our children. It is also not to imply that failure and sin don't hurt. Failing does hurt, but in the hurt comes the Healer.

Our children's failure isn't something to be scared of. It merely presents us the opportunity to teach them to build a relationship with Jesus Christ and use His Atoning power in their own lives. We teach them that the Atonement can heal a lie, bullying, a problem with pornography, or anything else they may encounter. Christ is bigger than them all.

> Failing does hurt, but in the hurt comes the Healer.

Consistently making it safe to

practice failure in our homes, we teach our children the security of a mother's love, the comforting that can come from the Holy Ghost, and the remarkable reach of the Atonement. We teach them resilience and, ultimately, where to go for help.

"Nevertheless, I know in whom I have trusted. My God hath been my support; he hath led me through mine afflictions in the wilderness; and he hath preserved me upon the waters of the great deep. He hath filled me with his love, even unto the consuming of my flesh. . . . O Lord, I have trusted in thee, and I will trust in thee forever."[55]

> Consistently making it safe to practice failure in our homes, we teach our children the security of a mother's love, the comforting that can come from the Holy Ghost, and the remarkable reach of the Atonement.

[55] 2 Nephi 4:19–21, 34.

Chapter 8
Finding Your Tribe

"Friendship is born at the moment when one person says to another 'What! You too? I thought I was the only one.'"

—C. S. Lewis

I am the product of many mothers. I was raised by my warrior of a single mother, but she didn't do it alone. She couldn't have. My gram; my aunts Diane and Kathryn; my great-aunt LaRae; my stepmother, Mary; my friends' moms; my Young Women leaders; and many other amazing women all contributed. Not a day will pass in which I don't identify little pieces of these women in myself.

Walking on the beach, I found an agate and remembered my grandmother, who, when I got bad news while we were on vacation, took me in her arms and let me cry a bit, then told me with love to not allow anything to steal the joy of the trip. When sitting down to help my daughter practice the piano, I say, "Don't get lazy hands! Imagine a tennis ball under your palms!" just like Aunt LaRae said to me while she attempted to teach me how to play the piano. (The poor woman attempted this task for six whole years before my stubbornness won the day. How I regret not being a pianist now!) As I work with the youth in my ward, I remember my Young Women leader Lisa, who took the time to go on a walk with me every week. It was much needed one-on-one attention that my working single mother could not give at that time. I even find myself humming the same line of a song over and over while cooking, just like my stepmother always did.

While my mother was and always will be the primary force of motherhood in my life, "I am a part of all that I have met."[56] I'm sure it was a comfort to my mother to know that in spite of the challenges her motherhood experience placed in her path, there were other women there to help.

When my children leave this home, they too will be a product of many mothers. They will be a product of their grammy's determination, their grandma's softness, their aunt Amber's consistency,

---

56 Alfred Lord Tennyson, "Ulysses" (1833).

their auntie Erin's joy, and I am so thankful for that. I can't do it alone, nor was I ever meant to.

As a mother, I am part of a tribe of women, a tribe that helps me mother and a tribe that supports each other in love. Defined specifically, the word *tribe* refers to a group descending from a common ancestor with a community of customs, traditions, and adherence to the same leader.[57] We belong to many tribes, though foremost is our Father's tribe. Collectively, we are the tribe of Mother Eve—mothers with a lineage of strength, virtue, and character, who have the power to sustain one another in our most sacred and holy calling of motherhood!

Our family spends a good deal of time in the Pacific Northwest where the air smells like pine and green and growth. Whenever we visit, we see a lot of fallen trees. Tim, our neighbor in the cottage we like to visit, carefully cuts these fallen trees into logs for his fireplace. I love looking at the rings on a cut tree. I find symbolism in them.

Think of your children at the center of the rings of a tree. The first ring around them is God. Then next is you (and their father, of course. The men in our children's lives are of the utmost importance, but for our purposes here, we will discuss

---

57 See dictionary.com.

the women). The ring after that is perhaps their grandmothers, then their aunts, and so on. In your situation, perhaps the rings are made up of different women. Some rings are closer to the children, and some are farther away, but every ring is a part of them. Every ring makes them strong.

It would be wise for us to remember that when we as women, as mother figures, interact with children who are not our own, we are adding a ring around their tree. Is it a ring that will add to their strength? Is it kind?

I spend much of my life interacting with children who are not my own. In 2015, I heard about a man named Chris Ulmer, a teacher who begins the day in his classroom by telling each student one by one something he loves about them. His simple message to each child is that they matter.

Inspired by this teacher, I decided to completely alter the way I interact with other people's children. I decided to conscientiously make them mine by being a mothering influence in their lives.

I teach acting, singing, and dancing to little children and have for many years. Motivated by great vision of potential, I decided to focus on the worth of the soul rather than progress. On the first day of class, I tell my students I don't care if they become perfect performers when the year ends, but I do care that when they leave the studio each week, they know how amazing they are. It is now my practice to end each of my classes five minutes early. I turn on the song "Bushel and a Peck" from the musical *Guys and Dolls*, and we have the same choreography each week as we sing the words to each other. Then I line them all up, and taking my cue from Chris Ulmer, as they leave, I tell them one by one something they did well.

This practice has completely revolutionized my classroom. The students' consistency on rehearsing at home has increased, kindness amongst students is significantly better, and they have naturally become stronger performers. All because of love.

This week, in my circle of influence, I will teach twenty-one students, interact with thirty-two young women in my Church calling, carpool eight children who are not my own, and rehearse a role for a play in which I am a mother to six children. In my mind, this means sixty-seven women are counting on me to be a part of their tribe. Sixty-seven women are trusting me to help them be the mother their children need.

When the carpool kids pile into my car, dubbed hilariously by one of them "the messiest car in the world," I try to take advantage of the time I have with them. I used to loathe carpools.

This week, in my circle of influence, I will teach twenty-one students, interact with thirty-two young women in my Church calling, carpool eight children who are not my own, and rehearse a role for a play in which I am a mother to six children. In my mind, this means sixty-seven women are counting on me to be a part of their tribe. Sixty-seven women are trusting me to help them be the mother their children need.

Now I try to see the occupants of my vehicle not as noisy, smelly responsibilities on my to-do list but instead as the precious children of another mother I have the privilege to drive from one place to another.

On the way to dance, I course-correct them when their topics of conversation aren't loving. I tell them they are fantastic when they think they "suck" after track practice. I praise their craft, sticky with Elmer's glue from preschool as "such a great job" while I buckle them into their car seats. And they aren't mine. They belong to sixty-seven other women and to God. But I am happy to do it because there are times like when my friend Debbie took my little girl to an audition for the school play and gave her a soda to celebrate when she was done. Debbie made my child feel amazing and stepped in for me when I needed help.

As the African proverb famously says, "It takes a village to raise a child." Our unique talents and gifts are needed to help raise the village. How comforting it is for me to send my daughter across the street to my neighbor Ashley for a physical, utilizing the many years of Ashley's education to become a health care professional. Likewise, I hope it is a relief for Ashley to send her daughter to my door so I can help her little girl prepare for an audition for the community musical.

This is what a tribe does. We put a lot of trust in each other. Yet, *are* we trusting one another? So many times, especially when I was beginning to mother, I thought good moms could do it all. Good moms didn't need help. But they do! This is substantiated in Ecclesiastes 4:9–10: "Two are better than one; because they have a good reward for their labour. For if they fall, the one will lift up his fellow: but woe to him that is alone when he falleth; for he hath not another to help him up." Sister, if you need to go to the dentist, don't do as I have done and sit the baby on your lap while getting a filling. No! Instead, call someone in the tribe. And when you come to pick up the baby after the dentist, bring your tribe mate a cupcake from her favorite bakery or some flowers from your yard. If you are brave and admit you need help, you give her permission to need you too. You allow her the blessings that come from service, blessings she may desperately need. Look at that scripture. *Woe*, it says. Don't do woe. Don't rob each other of being the tree rings, of being the village.

* * *

When I die, I intend to search out Marjorie Pay Hinckley and give her a hug. Her words have often saved me and reminded me that I am enough to be a mother. I feel that even though I never knew her, she is part of my tribe. On the topic of finding our tribe, Sister Hinckley has said, "We are all in this together. We need each other. Oh, how we need each other. Those of us who are old need you who are young, and hopefully, you who are young need some of us who are old. . . . We need deep and satisfying and loyal friendships with each other. These friendships are a necessary source of sustenance. We need to renew our faith every day. We need to lock arms and help build the kingdom so that it will roll forth and fill the whole earth."[58]

Sister Hinckley brings up another benefit of sisterhood so necessary to being the mothers our children need—it's friendship.

I have a lot of sisters. None of them are related to me. I grew up with four younger brothers but no other girls. And yet sisters surround me. I have sisters-in-law, neighbors, friends, ward members, book clubs, visiting teachers, cast mates, writing partners, workout buddies, yoga friends, coworkers, even fellow viewers of a reality show that shall not be named. And then, every once in awhile, a golden friend comes along—the kind of friend who really gets me and I her. These friendships are priceless, and I hold them close to my heart. I treasure all of my sisters, and I couldn't live without them.

Some in my tribe are of my same faith; some are not. Some have the same political ideas as I do; some do not. The melting pot of ideas and experiences is what makes my tribe of sisters amazing. All any of us really wants is to be seen.

---

58 *Glimpses* (Salt Lake City: Deseret Book Company, 1999), 254–55.

Friendship in motherhood is the ability to put aside whatever differing points of view we may have about parenting and see each other for the light we each bring to the world. Seeing another person and lifting her in no way diminishes our own light. Two lights together is only brighter light. We learned that in Primary! Even friendships that have left my life in the normal ebb and flow have taught me and helped make me a better mother.

Our grandmothers talked in their backyards while hanging laundry on the line. They shared recipes, laundry tips, and coupons. Not a lot has changed. We may do all of this via text, but the idea is the same. The tribe is the same.

I need to be clear that a tribe is not a clique. I don't believe in cliques. This is not to say I do not believe they exist; rather, I believe they *shouldn't* exist. Someone in my family used to say, "Add another cup of water to the soup." There is always room for one more in my tribe, and there should always be room for one more in yours as well.

There was a time in my life when I struggled to fit in. We'd just moved into a new neighborhood, and it didn't seem like there was room in anyone's tribe for one more. After quite a few weeks of feeling sorry for myself, I took it to the Lord, and He taught me what to do. When I went to church, I looked around for anyone sitting alone and tried to talk to them. Some of the women said, "This seat is saved," and asked me to move or got up and moved themselves. I kept trying. Eventually, I found a niche for myself with the empty nesters. These were wonderful women, and even though we weren't at the same stage in life, I fit with them. One of them taught me how to work on my family history, one of them shared books with me, and one of them swore like a sailor under her breath. I learned so much from them.

When it came time to move, I determined that I didn't know if I had been part of cliquey behavior before that time, but I knew I never would again. In my new neighborhood, I had an open-door policy to my heart that is still in effect to this day. If you need a place to be loved, there is always a place for you in my tribe.

Life in the tribe isn't always easy. Every blessing God gives us comes with an opportunity for growth. I have been offended and have myself offended the women in my tribe. Part of being in a tribe is tolerance, love, forgiveness, and boundaries. The Atonement is needed everywhere, and among our sisters is no exception. When I don't see eye to eye with another mom, I try to ask her something about her life, then I listen. Hearing another's story rarely leaves me without some kind of understanding. I may not agree with her, and I may not put her too close to my tender heart, but I will love her and work to understand her.

There have been times when it has been hard for me to embrace everyone. It's hard to hug a cactus. When that happens, I think of a line from *Hymns*, no. 235, "Should You Feel Inclined to Censure." It reads, "Those of whom we thought unkindly Oft become our warmest friends." This has been true for me in my life. Unlikely friend-ships are the most unexpected gifts. They are like getting the present you never knew you wanted, but now that you have it, you could never live without it.

Finding your tribe can be vulnerable. For instance, maybe you have gone to the park and seen the same woman and her child every day for three days. Your kids play well together, and she has been kind and warm in the few interactions you've had with her. What are you supposed to do? Walk up and say, "Hi, here I am. Do you want to be the person I call in the middle of the night because I ran out of baby Tylenol?" Yes. That is exactly what you are supposed to do. And have confidence because you know your worth.

Thanks to our membership in the Church, we have an automatic tribe of sisters in the Relief

Society. United in the cause of charity, it is a natural fit. I've always wanted this blessing to extend to those who are not of our faith and don't have a built-in tribe of sisters.

If you are aware of women around you in this situation, find them and reel them in. God has given them to you. Please don't do this so they can be part of your "mission plan" or because you think you'll feel good for doing missionary work. And, for heaven's sake, unless you know more than seven things about them or the Holy Ghost Himself instructs you, *do not* hand them a Book of Mormon right away. I've never enjoyed being anyone's project. Have you?

Instead, focus on their story. Who are they? What makes them tick? Why do they need you? And more importantly, why do you need them? We should love each other, not because it is one more step to climb on our proverbial stairway to heaven but because we are disciples of Jesus Christ and we love as He loves. He did not set out to fix people. He set out to love them so purely that they would fix themselves.

* * *

We bought our first house when I was only twenty-one years old. I was an eager young thing with a strong desire to put down roots and get

> We should love each other, not because it is one more step to climb on our proverbial stairway to heaven but because we are disciples of Jesus Christ and we love as He loves. He did not set out to fix people. He set out to love them so purely that they would fix themselves.

to work on life. There I was, a baby among all the women in my neighborhood. I spent hours preparing a very simple dessert for our first ward party. Being a social person, I don't normally worry about these things, but I literally shook with fear this time. This was my step from girl to grown woman. When I got to the social, I found that my fears were unfounded. A group of women surrounded me and fawned over my dessert. (I thought the dessert was extravagant at the time. It is now the dessert I make when I need to take something to Relief Society and have seven minutes to make it. That makes the attention those women showed me so much more poignant to me.) They enfolded me in their love, and I was safe. I was one of them.

Several months later, I had a baby. A woman I'd seen in the ward showed up with a gift from the Relief Society. Her name was Adrienne, and she became my mentor. She taught me the art of motherhood in a way no one else could. Our friendship has spanned fourteen years now. She is the one who, in her talk in the Relief Society meeting, gave me the mantra "You Are the Mother Your Children Need."

When Mary, the mother of Jesus, found herself engaged to Joseph and pregnant with the Savior of the world, she was full of wonder but perhaps a little fear at what the coming months would bring. Immediately, she sought a mentor—Elisabeth—who was herself miraculously pregnant.[59] God gave them something to bond over. Mary spent three months with her cousin in what I imagine was a cathartic sharing of pregnancy symptoms. God gave these cousins to each other.

I have had the privilege of learning from power-ful women mentors throughout my life. If you are a new mother, find a mentor. Don't feel bad ask-ing more experienced mothers for help, especially

59 See Luke 1.

if you do not have sisters or your own mother close by. Women a little more experienced than you will be happy to help. They didn't get where they are without help and will be there to support you.

If you are more experienced, be a mentor. There was a distinct time for me when I went from being one of the newest moms in my neighborhood to an average-experienced mom. It felt like an odd shift. I was comfortable with being taught, mentored, and guided. Then one day (and it happened faster than I would have thought), someone asked me for parenting advice. I became the mentor. The beautiful women who now seek my advice will be the ones to mentor my daughters in just a few years, so I am trying to mentor and love them well.

As I write the closing of this chapter, names, faces, and memories flash through my mind. I sit in a stupor of gratitude. My motherhood stands on the

> The beautiful women who now seek my advice will be the ones to mentor my daughters in just a few years, so I am trying to mentor and love them well.

shoulders of so many powerful women. All I can do is express gratitude to a gracious God who has given me so many sisters. It's such a glorious tribe.

Chapter 9
Saying No to the Mommy Wars

Associations between women can be like a line in a Charles Dickens' novel—"the best of times . . . the worst of times."[60] The blogosphere, parenting magazines, *The Washington Times*, talk shows, and even political candidates are all abuzz about mommy wars. As mothers, we are no strangers to these kinds of conflicts, groups of women banding together, proclaiming that their way of mothering is the right way and the rest of us can get a life. It sounds crazy. Typing the words *mommy wars* even looks crazy on the page. And yet . . . if we are honest with ourselves, haven't we all engaged in these wars in some way?

Have you ever had a thought like this: "There is a child walking barefoot! In. The. Road! Where

60 See *A Tale of Two Cities* (London: Chapman & Hall, 1859).

is that child's mother?" *(Mother of said child comes out of her house to find her child.)* "Finally! What is she doing? Is that a fruit snack? Is she giving this barefoot child sugar for a snack at 10:00 a.m.? And furthermore, is she in her bathrobe with her husband's snow boots on? Oh, that poor, poor child. He has a terrible mother. Thank heaven, she is taking him inside so I don't have to look at this train wreck anymore!"

Meanwhile, the bathrobe-clad, snow-booted mother has been up all night with a sick baby, and her toddler slipped out of the house while she was changing a diaper. In a hurry to get him back into the house, she grabbed the first pair of shoes she saw—her husband's snow boots. Attempting to coax her child back inside where the sick baby is crying, she offered the fruit snack that was in the pocket of her robe. She is tired and wants to cry.

As "good" mothers, we have opinions about everything. Education, vaccination, breastfeeding, diapering, electronic usage, extracurricular activities, eating habits, spiritual practices, and on and on . . . forever. Why? Why, when our goal is the same, do we automatically put ourselves at odds with those who should be our compatriots?

Articles expounding on the mommy wars are plentiful. People with PhDs and LCSWs, clergy, bloggers, moms, writers, and doctors all contribute. As I've studied many of the articles in detail, I've found a common thread running through each of them. One predominant issue is keeping us at war with each other: it is the feeling of our own inadequacy. Lauded researcher of shame and vulnerability, Dr. Brené Brown has said, "One of the reasons we judge each other so harshly in this world of parenting is because . . . we perceive anyone else who's doing anything differently than what we're doing as criticizing our choices." If someone criticizes our choices, it must mean we are in some way inadequate. If we are inadequate, how will our children make it through this life and ultimately back to their heavenly home? The feeling of inadequacy is too much for most of us to take. Too vulnerable. Too scary. And so we judge back. We tell ourselves we are right. We run as fast as we can away from that scary feeling of inadequacy and straight into the arms of judging others.

In a brilliant marketing campaign, Similac recently released an online video entitled "Mother Hood." The clip begins with different groups of moms clumped together. They stare at each other and make comments, insinuating that their way of mothering is the right way and that the others are wrong. As the tension increases between these groups of moms (and one group of dads), a mother lets go of the handle of her stroller. The stroller and the baby inside begin to roll away from the unaware mother. Suddenly these sparring groups drop everything and run to the baby rolling perilously down a steep and treacherous hill. In an instant, they are united in purpose—to save a child in danger. At the bottom of the hill, the baby is safe. The mothers look at each other and comfort the escaped baby's mom, then begin to shake hands and introduce themselves to one another. The silliness of their contention fades as their shared experience reveals the truth: a child was in danger, and that child could have been theirs. They are more alike than different. Words across the screen read "No matter what our beliefs, we are parents first. Welcome to the Sisterhood of Motherhood."

The sisterhood of motherhood—what a joyous concept!

When inadequacy comes to the surface, tempting us to judge another mother, we have a choice. We can continue in silent, audible, or written judgment in an effort to hide our fear of imperfection, or we can lean into the imperfection. Often, we believe that if *someone else* is right, *we* must be wrong or vice versa. My sisters, what if we are all right? What if there are many right choices in mothering? What if in *my* belief, kids should be in bed at 8:00 p.m., and in *your* belief, they should self-govern their bed-time? Are both parenting styles right? And what if the question as to right and wrong styles of mother-ing really isn't any of our business anyway? What if it belongs solely to the mom and her Lord?

In 1993, Sister Okazaki stood at the pulpit of the Tabernacle in Salt Lake City and held up two very different quilts. She said, "There's not one right way to be a quilt as long as the pieces are stitched together firmly. Both of these quilts will keep us warm and cozy. Both are beautiful and made with love. There's not just one right way to be a Mormon woman, either, as long as we are firmly grounded in faith in the Savior, make and keep covenants, live the commandments, and work together in charity."[61]

I know I am failing in so many ways, but I'm also succeeding in a lot of areas in my motherhood experience. I'm going to choose to believe the same is true of you. I believe that someday each of us mothers will kneel at the feet of our Savior as we talk to Him about being a mom, and we are going to lament with broken hearts all of the things we did wrong, and He will make them right.

So in the meantime, unless we are saving an-other mommy's baby's life, let's all just keep our focus on our own baby carriages, shall we?

---

61 "Strength in the Savior," *Ensign*, November 1993.

I believe that someday each of us mothers will kneel at the feet of our Savior as we talk to Him about being a mom, and we are going to lament with broken hearts all of the things we did wrong, and He will make them right.

Chapter 10
A Word on the Fathers

My sister-in-law Erin and I went to see a documentary about empowering women to love their bodies. As we left the theater, I couldn't wait to talk with her about it, but I looked at her and could tell she was troubled. Her brow was doing this furrowing thing it does when she is bothered. I thought her reaction was odd, as it was such an impactful film on womanhood, something I would normally expect her to love.

She said she liked the movie. As a woman, she left feeling powerful, but she was upset by the image of men presented in the film. "I get that we need to empower women," she said, "but as a mother to only boys, I am concerned. Where are the movies that tell my sons they are enough? Where are the films that portray them as the good guys? Where are the masses of people concerned about my boys' self-image? And if this is the level they are taught to attain, how will they rise?"

Her response gave me pause. The conclusion we came to was that just because a movie empowered women, it didn't necessarily mean it was discrediting men. However, we also jointly concurred that there was a definite need in the industry for more media aimed at empowering men.

After chatting more about the film, we each left to face the mom's-been-gone-to-a-movie-all-night chaos in our respective homes. I had a long drive home from the movie theater, and as I drove, Erin's thoughts swirled in my own mind. This was the second girl-power movie she and I had been to in as many months. As I thought over the other movie we had gone to see—a chick-flick—I was appalled at the message it sent about men. I was ashamed that as a wife and mother of a young son, I hadn't even caught those messages the way she had. Once I noticed it that night, I began to see it everywhere: social media, TV, movies, video games, everywhere.

The media wants to present men as "less" than women, as if respecting them somehow diminishes women. I join my voice with that of Elder D. Todd Christofferson in saying, "We call on media and entertainment outlets to portray devoted and capable fathers who truly love their wives and intelligently guide their children, instead of the bumblers and buffoons or 'the guys who cause problems,' as fathers are all too frequently depicted."[62] As the media does all they can to demean men, we must do all we can to build them up.

In order to be the mothers our children need, we must respect our children's fathers. We cannot forget that they too were divinely appointed to our children, and they have a sacred role. It is important to nurture our relationships with our children's fathers.

> In order to be the mothers our children need, we must respect our children's fathers. We cannot forget that they too were divinely appointed to our children, and they have a sacred role.

In ideal circumstances, we would experience this relationship of mother/father with our husbands, but sometimes it is not an ideal world.

62 "Fathers," *Ensign*, May 2016.

No matter our circumstances, we can still offer respect. My college roommate and I shared the experience of divorced parents. Both of her parents were local to our university, and I was always surprised at how they treated each other. When it came to my roommate, they were unitedly there for her. They jointly attended her university choir concerts, and they respected each other in their coparenting responsibilities. One night after my roommate went through a break-up, I came home to find both of her parents comforting her on our couch. When she asked one parent if she could go to California for spring break, they would not answer without consulting the other parent. I learned from them that coparenting in a divorce situation is possible and can even be beautiful. I recognize that my roommate was lucky to have two parents committed to parenting this way, and that may not be your situation. Where none of us can control everything, we can control how we speak about our child's father, especially to our children.

In marriage, it is not *either/or*; it is *and*. Your shining does not diminish your husband's and vice versa. When two people are committed to each other, there is give and take in the responsibilities and rewards of parenting. This dance, when executed with two willing hearts, is amazing to watch. Experiencing it is among the most treasured gifts of my life.

I was a teenager when Mike Wallace interviewed the prophet, President Hinckley, for the television show *60 Minutes*. In the interview, President Hinckley said, "The men hold the priesthood, yes. But my wife is my companion. In this Church the man neither walks ahead of his wife nor behind his wife but at her side. They are coequals in this life in a great enterprise."

On our wedding day in the Mount Timpanogos temple, the priesthood holder who sealed my

In marriage, it is not either/or; it is and. Your shining does not diminish your husband's and vice versa. When two people are committed to each other, there is give and take in the responsibilities and rewards of parenting. This dance, when executed with two willing hearts, is amazing to watch.

husband and me for all eternity offered some wise counsel: He told Doug to kneel with me in prayer that night and to pray earnestly for my welfare; the night after that, I was to pray fervently for Doug's welfare. "Never miss a night," he said. We took his advice and, excepting the times we are traveling separately, have never missed a night.

I am the mother my children need because Doug is the father our children need. I know that if called upon, I could do it without him, but I was never meant to. When I respect and honor my husband as my coequal, it in no way diminishes me. In doing so, I teach Doug how I would like him to respect and honor me. I teach my daughters how to offer respect to boys now and to their future husbands later. And I teach my son that he is not some fool to be mocked on television or in the movies. He is not ruled by the instincts of his body, as is so often portrayed. I show him that he too is of infinite worth.

In every circumstance, I have faith that Heavenly Father is the Father we all need. He gives us direct access to Him through prayer. He is always there and is *always* what we need.

In every circumstance, I have faith that Heavenly Father is the Father we all need. He gives us direct access to Him through prayer. He is always there and is always what we need.

Chapter 11
"But If Not . . ."

I remember that I was holding my baby daughter when I first heard Elder Dennis E. Simmons's conference talk in April 2004 entitled "But If Not." His talk related the story of Shadrach, Meshach, and Abednego found in Daniel 3. These three were brought before King Nebuchadnezzar, who demanded that they worship false idols or be thrown into a fire and burned alive. Shadrach, Meshach, and Abednego exercised great faith that Father in Heaven would not suffer them to be burned. And then, furthering the example of their faith, they went on to say that, yes, they believed they would be spared, "but if not" (Daniel 3:18), they would still believe.

This story and Elder Simmons's talk made a huge impression on me. Faith is a beautiful thing in ideal circumstances, but what about the "but if not" moments in our lives? Having faith in those moments isn't just beautiful—it is exquisite. Elder Simmons said, "We must understand that great challenges make great [women]. We don't seek tribulation, but if we respond in faith, the Lord strengthens us. The *but if nots* can become remarkable blessings."[63]

We are striving to be the best possible mothers we can be. But what about the "but if nots"? Situations resulting from our choices or others' choices, such as divorce, death, addiction, abuse, depression, single parenting, infertility, medical issues, and countless others of life's challenges, can lead us to question if we really can be the mothers our children need. These challenges can result from intentional acts or can simply happen as part of our life experiences. No matter how they come, we are often left in their aftermath, not knowing what to do and firmly believing there is no way we are enough for what our children need.

Am I the Mother My Children Need?

Even in the most normal of life's circumstances, just by being a mom, you are going to feel like you aren't enough. Inadequacy is going to come for a visit. A hundred times. A thousand times.

---

63 "But If Not," *Ensign*, May 2004.

Probably more. You will decide the baby probably isn't very sick only to take her to the hospital three days later with pneumonia. The dentist may roll his eyes at you when he pronounces that your son has four—yes, four—cavities. Your ten-year-old may not speak with you for three days because you forgot to come to "moms and muffins" day at school even though she told you about it every day for three weeks. And you may never know what you have done to deserve the symphony of slamming doors from your teenager. You are going to scream when they don't deserve it, forget important things, feed them too much processed food, say yes when you should say no, say no when you should say yes, and make scores of bad judgment calls along the way.

When my daughter was three years old, she approached me one day with light in her twinkly brown eyes. I was approximately eight million years pregnant. She tugged on my tent of a shirt and said, "Mommy, come see! I'm so excited!"

We had just gotten a new high-gloss piano. I had a special "in" on the piano and had been able to buy it for wholesale, but it was still a very expensive investment for our little family. Working a sales job from home, I had made a bigger-than-normal sale and used my commission check to buy it. It was the only brand-new thing I had ever owned. Everything else was from yard sales or had been handed down.

My daughter led me by the hand to the piano, where she proudly showed the evidence of a new skill she had acquired: writing her name. There was my beautiful, three-day-old piano with the letters H-A-I-L-E-Y etched clear through its high-gloss finish and into the wood with the metal end of a bobby pin.

I lost my mind. In my fury, I put her in her room and told her she was very naughty and I didn't want to see her for the rest of the day. I yelled till my throat hurt and slammed the door.

Then I got out my suitcase and started packing. I called my husband at work and told him he had better come home because I'd had it and was leaving this life in favor of my alternate reality—I was headed to New York. He carefully pointed out that he didn't think there were any casting calls for pregnant Mormon housewives on Broadway and I should probably take my giant belly to bed for awhile.

My sweet girl didn't know she had done anything wrong. She was excited to show me she was proficient at a skill I had taught her! She and I had spent hours at the counter practicing the letters of her name. That night, after my husband had put her to bed, I stared at her fuzzy head and sweet lips. I felt awful, but I was still so sad about my piano. I knew we didn't have the money to repair it.

When I recounted my sad tale to my husband's grandmother the next week, she told me to be happy that I couldn't afford to replace or fix the scratches. She said that someday I would come to love the letters on the piano. Then she told me a story of her own daughter, Kathy, who had painted her name with nail polish on a newly painted bathroom wall.

It was in the middle of World War II when paint was impossible to come by. A neighbor had given Grandma the paint left over from their own painting job. There was just enough to paint the tiny bathroom. The rest of their house remained bare-walled. Grandma was so angry at her little girl.

She and Grandpa didn't find the money to paint over the nail polish until the 1970s, and she was so excited to finally be rid of the polish that had always bothered her. Smiling and satisfied, she finished the new paint job. Then she looked at the wall where the tiny letters K-A-T-H-Y had been, and paintbrush still wet, Grandma sat on the bathroom floor and wept with regret for having painted over it. Kathy was now a grown woman, and Grandma felt she had just painted over a little piece of her baby girl whom she missed.

I thought it was a sweet story, but at the time, I couldn't imagine feeling that way about my piano!

A decade has passed. So has Grandma. We use our piano every day, and every day I see those little letters. The girl who etched them is closer to leaving my home than she is to being that toddler. And how I ache for putting my toddler in her room and breaking her spirit! I wish I could have been better for her—I wish I could have been more.

I know we think we can do more than we are doing now and that we could have been better for our children in the past. But is that really true? Consider this: "For we know that it is by grace that we are saved, after all we can do."[64] If you are like me, you sometimes stay up at night wondering what else you possibly could have done and clearly seeing in hindsight that you could have done so much better. You tell yourself why you don't deserve grace. In her book *Amazed by Grace*, Sheri L. Dew wrote, "'After all we can do' is not about a to-do list. It has very little to do with quantity or output. Jesus Christ is the only one to ever walk this earth who did all that could be done in mortality. Instead, doing all we can do is

---

64   2 Nephi 25:23.

about the direction we're headed and what kind of men and women we are becoming. There is nothing simple about this, because it isn't natural for the natural man or woman to want to do good or be good."[65]

Mothering is hard, but would you give any of it up? If the answer to that question is no, then that is enough. YOU are enough. We have within us the divine potential to be the mother our children need. Living so we are moving toward that potential and utilizing the Atonement are what make us enough.

In addition to our own self-questioning, there is the little principle of agency that comes around to make us feel inadequate. I've often said tongue-in-cheek that as a mom, I can see how Satan's plan makes a lot of sense! No agency means no pressure. Wouldn't

> Mothering is hard, but would you give any of it up? If the answer to that question is no, then that is enough. YOU are enough.

---

65 *Amazed by Grace* (Salt Lake City: Deseret Book Company, 2015), 43–44.

we all love to force our children to choose the right? "No," you say? You just haven't had a teenager yet! Get back to me on that one.

Joking aside, you may do everything with textbook perfection and may still watch your teenager suffer with drug addiction. Your adult child may choose to deviate from the principles you so carefully taught her in her youth. In this world of agency, we may feel completely out of control and wonder why giving our children everything we had was, in our own view, just not enough.

Consider my friend Allie*: Allie couldn't have been a better mother. She taught the gospel in her home. She was invested in her two children's lives; her world revolved around them. And then one ordinary day in their ordinary lives, someone the family loved and trusted hurt Allie's son . . . and he didn't tell a soul. In an effort to escape the pain of his experience, Allie's precious boy turned to drugs to cope. The family poured every penny they could spare into rehabilitation. They did everything they could think to do. The pain and grief of addiction took a toll on the family in every way, ultimately resulting in Allie's son's early death.

In spite of it all, she couldn't keep her precious boy safe from those who sought to do harm, and she couldn't even spare his life.

She believed her son would be saved. But if not, could she still believe?

The adversary is a cunning and smart foe of mothers. He uses a seemingly endless arsenal of tools, such as pornography, deceit, shame, temptation, and addiction to separate children from the love of their mothers and to separate mothers from the love of their Father in Heaven.

But perhaps his most effective tool is tempting good-hearted women to question their own adequacy and efficacy, thus tempting them to refuse grace for themselves. This is something we simply cannot allow for ourselves. We must choose grace.

I have faith that you have within you all you need to mother your children; however, if the "but if not" moments come, will you allow the grace of our Savior's Atonement to save you?

Allie's family is adjusting to life without their son and brother. And the grief is significant. But Allie knows where her son is . . . and whom he is with. She knows that in his death, he has been saved from the prison of his private pain and addictions and now, separated from the ability to feed those addictions, is free to progress. She refuses to question her adequacy as a mother. Within her most honest thoughts, she knows she was just the right mother for her son. And she loved him in exactly the way he needed her to love him. She still loves him. She has expressed to Father in Heaven and her son a deep desire to be able to experience the relationship with him from the other side that she has missed having with him here on earth.

Are All Mothers the Mothers Their Children Need?

When contemplating being the mother our children need, perhaps some are led to ask the question, "If I am the mother my children need, why didn't I get the mother I needed?" Challenging experiences in our family of origin can lead us to question the belief that divinity is within us all. In experiencing this earthly life with these earthly challenges, there are times when we just cannot understand why we weren't given what we feel we needed or even deserved to have from our childhood experience.

There is great redemption to be found in the—sometimes lifelong—process of forgiveness. Forgiveness for many of the things we see in our own upbringing as failures comes more easily as we ourselves experience our own parenting imperfections. We become one with our mothers. I have called my mother many times to say, "Hey, Mom, you were right," or "Hey, Mom, I know

I've always given you sass about not taking me into the doctor for three days after I broke my foot, but I'm sitting here with my own daughter, and, gosh, mom, she is being so dramatic. I don't know if her foot is broken. Maybe you didn't know either." These are normal experiences and can bond new moms to their own mothers.

Yet there are times when the experiences in our childhood fall outside the boundaries of normal. Some of us mothers experienced seriously difficult situations in our youth. If this is you, there is hope. When the Spirit testifies to you that the time is right, consider joining the path of forgiveness. In his beautiful book entitled *The Book of Forgiving: The Fourfold Path for Healing Ourselves and Our World*, Anglican Bishop Desmond Tutu poignantly states, "The one who offers forgiveness as a grace, is immediately untethered from the yoke that bound him or her to the person who caused the harm. When you forgive, you are free to move on in life, to grow, to no longer be a victim. When you forgive, you slip the yoke, and your future is unshackled from your past."[66]

Building on Anglican Bishop Tutu's words, when through the Atonement of Jesus Christ we

---

66 *The Book of Forgiving: The Fourfold Path for Healing Ourselves and Our World* (New York City: HarperOne, 2015).

are free from the shackles of our past challenges, we find quick access to peace. This is the peace that comes when we see the divine nature within ourselves, thus allowing us to be more of what our own children need. What kind of real estate is your pain taking up in your soul? Imagine what you could fill yourself with if the pain were evicted from that precious and valuable property!

If you feel you did not have the childhood experiences you needed, and perhaps had some experiences you definitely didn't need, the Atonement is for you! You can rise above! Do all you can to come to know that the heartache and hurt you experienced was never God's plan for your life. Although your pain wasn't His plan, He knew that through His gift of agency, you could possibly be hurt through the actions of others. And so, included in His plan was the provision of a Savior! He sent Jesus Christ to atone for each of us as well as those who wrong us so we can heal from the hurt.

As you seek to magnify your role as mother, you can heal. Many valuable tools are there to assist you in the process: medical and psychological assistance, Church leaders, temples, spiritual guides, angelic companionship, good books, healthy habits, scriptures, using your talents, people who surround you, and many more. Ultimately, in all of these things, it is the power of the Atonement that heals. There is great redemption in being capable to give to your children what you did not get in your own childhood experience.

Others of us may ask why women who make choices that don't seem to reflect the desire for motherhood seem to easily bear children, while conception is difficult and sometimes impossible for some who feel they would make wonderful parenting choices. Those mothers

> There is great redemption in being capable to give to your children what you did not get in your own childhood experience.

couldn't possibly be "the mother their children need," could they?

Are all mothers the mother their children need? It might be difficult for some, but the answer to the question is yes. Our divinity is inherent. Our motherhood was divinely appointed prior to our birth and is part of who we are as women. Consider this beautiful reminder from

President Uchtdorf:

> I am not suggesting that we accept sin or overlook evil, in our personal life or in the world. Nevertheless, in our zeal, we sometimes confuse sin with sinner, and we condemn too quickly and with too little compassion. We know from modern revelation that "the worth of souls is great in the sight of God." We cannot gauge the worth of another soul any more than we can measure the span of the universe. Every person we meet is a VIP to our Heavenly Father. Once we understand that, we can begin to understand how we should treat our fellowmen.

> One woman who had been through years of trial and sorrow said through her tears, "I have come to realize that I am like an old 20-dollar bill—crumpled, torn, dirty, abused, and scarred. But I am still a 20-dollar bill. I am worth something. Even though I may not

> look like much and even though I
> have been battered and used, I am
> still worth the full 20 dollars."[67]

There was once a man who sought to destroy the Church. His heart was hardened, and he led many away through his charm, flattery, and cunning. There was also a man who was one of the greatest missionaries of his time. He wore his life out in the service of God. We study and revere his ministry. Both of these men are, of course, Alma the Younger. Within Alma was the natural man with the propensity to do evil, but there was also the divine potential to do and be good. His heart was softened. He was changed. But let us not forget that before the change, he was struck down by an angel and rendered comatose. The change wasn't quick and easy. Ultimately, Alma chose his divine potential. Similarly, Paul, the sons of Mosiah, and countless others throughout time have chosen to live up to their potential.

The choices we make regarding the type of mothers we will be are our own, as they were for our mothers before us. Our divine nature insists that we are the mothers our children need, but whether we live up to that potential is a choice we each must

---

67 "You Are My Hands," *Ensign*, May 2010.

make. No matter our past experiences or mistakes, no matter how we have wronged or been wronged, there is hope in a bright and joyful future with our families. Elder Holland reminds us, "However late you think you are, however many chances you think you have missed, however many mistakes you feel you have made or talents you think you don't have, or however far from home and family and God you feel you have traveled, I testify to you that you have not traveled beyond the reach of divine love. It is not possible for you to sink lower than the infinite light of Christ's Atonement."[68]

> When we stand before the Lord one day, we will account for our agency. Yes, this life may have given us challenges, but with the light of Christ's Atonement, did we rise?

When we stand before the Lord one day, we will account for our agency. Yes, this life may have given us challenges, but with the light of Christ's Atonement, did we rise?

In those "but if not" moments when the world

---

68 "The Laborers in the Vineyard," *Ensign*, May 2012.

feels claustrophobic—collapsing in around us—
when we feel like we have failed or been failed
and our very humanity or the humanity of others has been a detriment to the mothering of our
precious children, we must make a conscious
choice to stop. Wherever we are, whatever we
are doing, stop. Come back to the center. Our
Heavenly Parents and our Savior Jesus Christ are
the center, and their love is a safe place to return
to, even in the midst of motherhood's most sobering trials. There is peace there. This is where we will find our worth again. We must fall to our knees in prayer, then stop for a moment and feel God's love for us personally. Drink deeply from the well of His love, and

> Our Heavenly Parents and our Savior Jesus Christ are the center, and their love is a safe place to return to, even in the midst of motherhood's most sobering trials. There is peace there. This is where we will find our worth again.

you can find the strength to be Mom again to-morrow.

Know that this center place is always inside of you, even when you don't have the strength to consciously access it. Within this holy place is the love of heaven and the support of *your team*. Listen to the silent voices of the women who came before you and are telling you that you are enough. These are powerful, righteous, perfectly imperfect mothers whose legacies have spilled down the generations of time, beginning with our Heavenly Mother, flowing to mother Eve, and so on all the way to you, in this moment, on your knees in humble prayer.

He will deliver us, but if the "but if not" moment happens and we are called upon to face the worst, may we remember that our Savior said, "I will not leave you comfortless: I will come to you."[69] Our Brother is with us. Our ancestor mothers are with us. And we are with each other.

You are not alone. You are your divine potential, and you *are* the mother your children need.

---

69 John 14:18.

You are not alone. You are your divine potential, and you are the mother your children need.

Epilogue
You Are the Mother Your Children Need

It's 12:26 a.m., and I am just finishing writing for the night. Saturday was a regular day. I'm exhausted. I got after the kids way too much today. I also loved them with ease, distributing many hugs and kisses as needed. Christian, my four-year-old, and I had a tickle war today, and then when I got him out of his car seat, he put his arms around my neck and his legs around my waist. Hailey, age thirteen, and Libby, age nine, were walking ahead of us into the house, and I realized I don't remember the last time either of them wrapped their bodies around me. So I tried to memorize the feeling of Christian's grubby arms rubbing the back of my neck, his fingers tangled in my hair.

"I love you to all of the planets, Mamma," he said into my ear as I was putting him down. Into the house we walked, to the laundry piles and the piano practicing, and the cooking dinner. For a moment, it felt like my time slowed as my life's reality whirled around at regular speed. My home. My people. My sacred chaos.

> And at the end of my life when my accomplishments are listed, none . . . not any . . . will top the titles of wife and mother.

Being a mother isn't just something I do. It is in *everything* I do. Being a mother is on the stage with me when I act, at the pulpit when I speak, on the computer screen when I write, and in the classes I teach. Being a mother influences my political ideals, my civic participation, and my life's work. It is who I am. And at the end of my life when my accomplishments are listed, none . . . not any . . . will top the titles of wife and mother.

Tomorrow has become today in the waning moments of my writing, and it is now the Sabbath. I look forward to taking the sacrament. I look forward to renewing my covenants. I look forward to thanking Father in Heaven for the gift it is to be in the throes of motherhood. Life as a mom is imperfect, hard, messy, and heartbreakingly painful. It is also stretching, enlightening, fun, and full of joyful holiness.

Each time I have sat to write this book, I have prayed before starting. I pray that my mind will be clear. I pray that the words He would have you know will find their way to the page. I pray that somehow my focus will remain steady despite my four-year-old smacking my leg repeatedly with a toy car and my thirteen-year-old practicing the trumpet (otherwise known as making dying-elephant noises) in the other room, and my nine-year-old dancing with the dog. But mostly I pray that you will believe me when I say *You are the mother your children need*. My prayer always ends with, "Father, help me believe I am too."

I know I'm never going to be a perfect mom, but I know that all Father in Heaven requires of me to be the mother my children need is to show up *as me* with Him.

I'm going to try. Care to join me?

Acknowledgments

I have felt the wind of so many people at my back, pushing me along my way as I have written this book. I pause to thank them.

Many thanks to the entire Covenant publishing team for believing that I had something to share and helping to execute the vision. To my editor, Samantha (Sam) Millburn, upon whom the whole of the finished product rests . . . it is exactly what I hoped it would be. To Kathy Gordon and the rest of the editing team. To Margaret Weber-Longoria, Christina Marcano, and the graphics department for their beautiful design work. To Blair Leishman and Phil Reschke for their work on the audiobook, Tammy Kolkman for your work on sales, and Stephanie Lacy for your work on promotion. To Robby Nichols, Verl Sabey, Susan Condie, Doug Gardiner, and Jennifer Busenbark. Deep appreciation to the tireless working teams of retailers (*I see you!*) who have put this book in the hands of readers! To Caitlyn Connoly, whose artistic vision covers this book and consistently inspires mothers to be fierce defenders of their children.

Which brings me to you, my dear readers and fellow moms. Thanks for hanging out with me for a few pages. And thank you most of all for showing up as you with God. You inspire me to be a better mother.

Thanks to my writing groups, book clubs, Relief Society sisters, women with whom I have served in Church callings, *The Living Room* podcast, Utah COPA coworkers, my yoga gurus, and my many fellow actors and production staffs. To my tribe of powerful women friends all over the world, whether your stories or names are mentioned in this book or not, my mothering is a part of you. I treasure you.

To President Scott L. Livingston and Dr. Jonathan G. Sandberg. You have been angels on this earth, and I am forever grateful.

Thanks to my parents: Jane, Jeff, Mary, John, and Leila. To my siblings: Robert, Erin, Andrew, Morgan, Kyrsti, David, John, Amber, Thomas, April, Sarah, Ben, and their kids. To Beva and Paula. To my extended family.

I cannot repay the mothers who have shaped my world and inspired these pages: Heavenly Mother, Jane Bell Meyer—mom, Suzanne Wilson McKay, Leila Gardiner, Nina Hansen, LaRae Wilson, Erin Axson, Amber Gardiner, Mary Axson, Kathryn Bell, Diane Schultz, Sarah Gardiner, April Gardiner, and all those who have stepped in when I've needed a mothering influence. My thanks, reverence, and love.

My most deep and unending gratitude to my best friends and champions: the love of my heart, Doug Gardiner, and the children who gave me the title of mom: Hailey, Elisabeth, and Christian.

Finally, most humbly, I offer my thanks to my Heavenly Father and my Brother, Jesus Christ. I know you are with me all the time. And "I can do all things through Christ which strengtheneth me."[70]

---

70 Philippians 4:13.

About the Author

Christie Gardiner treasures her roles as wife and mother. As a writer, she has worked as a blogger for the Utah Jazz and served as director of brand journalism for Illume Gallery of Fine Art. Christie has enjoyed participating in speaking engagements all over the state and loves reminding groups of women that with the Savior, they're not alone. Her performing career has spanned three decades in theater, television, film, commercials, podcasting, and voiceover work. She is a longtime faculty member at the Utah Conservatory of Performing Arts (Utah COPA), where she loves inspiring young people to increase their self-esteem through participation in the arts. In her spare time, she can be found with her children in nature or on their yoga mats. She currently serves in the Young Women organization.

Christie lives in the shadow of a temple in Pleasant Grove, Utah, and occasionally in Cannon Beach, Oregon, with her husband, Doug, their three children, Hailey, Elisabeth, and Christian, as well as their dog, Jack. Look for her at www.christiegardiner.com.

For a complete bibliography, including all of the author's resources and references on this topic, please visit the author's website, where a reading group guide and additional study materials are available.